Dr. Daniel A. Langer

Prof. Dr. Oliver P. Heil (Ph.D.)

Luxury Essentials

Essential Insights and Strategies to Manage Luxury Products

Scottsdale and Mainz: January 2015

University of Mainz, Center for Research on Luxury

This book provides truly new insights into the seemingly elusive concept of luxury and it does so using a compact and convenient format. More precisely, it condenses the authors' groundbreaking book on Luxury: Marketing & Management - which has become a standard textbook on luxury and is used in Universities around the world - into easy to digest pieces of knowledge, yet maintains the essence of the full-fledged original. Thus, the Essentials provide the best format for people on the go yet provide a comprehensive entry into this fascinating world of luxury with its most unique products, ideas and challenges for consumers, managers and also scientists.

This is what the world's leading experts on luxury say about the authors' book "Luxury: Marketing & Management":

"The book Luxury: Marketing & Management will be of considerable interest to both managers and academics seeking to understand and manage luxury goods in the 21st Century."
Prof. Dr. David B. Montgomery, Stanford University & former Dean, Singapore Management University

"This new and interesting research provides insight into the unique world of luxury and I have no doubt will prove a fascinating read for consumers and managers. Rolls-Royce Motor Cars has been at the pinnacle of automotive luxury for over 100 years and it is enlightening to see scientific research on the industry."
Torsten Müller-Ötvös, CEO Rolls-Royce Motor Cars Ltd

"This book provides a large coverage of research on luxury, combined with new practical approaches, such how to analyze the luxury potential of a category on the basis of the price differentials. Very enlightening reading for managers and consumers alike."
Prof. Dr. Gilles Laurent, HEC Paris

"Many asked me in the course of the year what is the essence of luxury, and there is in my opinion a one world answer to this: luxury is pure emotion. In their book the authors provide an elaborated overview on luxury both from a researcher's and a manager's perspective. It's a must-read for those interested in luxury."
Pietro Beccari, Chairman & CEO Fendi

"As a maker of high-end mechanical watches, we are impressed by the precision of this analysis on the meaning of luxury today and the practical and valuable conclusions for a successful management of luxury products. Most interesting work!"
Philippe Merk, CEO Audemars Piguet

"This book's development of luxury signals provides a new and creative perspective of luxury. Reading it will amount to a very good investment for managers and be enlightening for consumers of luxury items around the globe. Fun to read!"
Prof. Dr. Kris Helsen, Hong Kong University of Science & Technology (HKUST)

Daniel André Langer is founder and CEO of ÉQUITÉ, a leading brand strategy firm, where he advises some of the most important premium and luxury brands around the world. He is one of the world's most renowned experts on the management of luxury brands. The author holds a Ph.D. and a Masters degree from the University of Mainz. He also studied in Madrid and attended executive education at Harvard, IESE and Thunderbird. He held several top management positions in Europe, Japan and USA for Henkel, L'Oréal and Nestlé, among those leading Henkel's North American Beauty Care division to all time high results. He is author of several top-rated management books, won multiple prestigious marketing awards and is a sought-after commentator by the media including the Economist. Dr. Langer's research focuses on deepening our understanding of luxury. Importantly, the marketing of regular products can benefit substantially from luxury research findings in terms of identifying different and creative strategies enhancing innovativeness, competitiveness and profitability of fast moving consumer goods. Learn more at www.equiteconsulting.com.

Oliver Heil is the Chaired Professor of Marketing at the Johannes Gutenberg-University of Mainz (Germany). He holds a Ph.D. as well as a Masters degree from the University of Pennsylvania's Wharton School. The author taught at Wharton, UCLA, IU, Lingnan and HKUST. His publications appeared in leading scientific journals and he co-authored several books. As the recipient of various academic honors he currently serves on several boards and lectures on a variety of topics. Prof. Heil is working on identifying optimal sizes and formats for limited editions of luxury products and identifying causal factors of luxury design. Also, he is working on applying the luxury index toward regular products such as fast moving consumer goods as well as luxury products to enhance branding strategies. Prof. Heil is organizing a global luxury event bringing together managers, researchers and customers dealing with luxury products. Learn more at www.luxury-research.org.

Table of Contents

Table of Contents (With Subheadings)

Preface

Whether we teach luxury to students or have discussions with luxury professionals or talk to luxury consumers, one common theme emerges again and again: While luxury seems to be easy to grasp at first, it quickly evolves into a most complicated endeavor. That is, its management poses most unique challenges, e.g. as price is often seemingly irrelevant. While intuitively there should be a lot of publications on luxury that really matter, there are only a few that try to meet the luxury challenge.

With this in mind we conducted extensive research on luxury during recent years and founded a unique University research institute, the Center for Research on Luxury at the Johannes Gutenberg-University of Mainz with the ambition to provide breakthrough insights about luxury and take research, publications and management insights of luxury to the next level.

This book has the ambition to provide what many call the "gold standard" in luxury publications "Luxury: Marketing & Management" (Langer & Heil 2013) to a much broader audience. It covers the key content in an essential, more compact, easy to digest format. To those who want to go beyond the essentials and get additional inspiration by more background and more examples, the original textbook would seem to be a natural next step to read.

It is difficult to define luxury, since many people think of it in different ways. It is not necessarily related to simply the price of something. For the wealthy it may be the purchase of an ultra-expensive piece of clothing or bottle of champagne, but for poorer people it may be something as simple as being able to afford a better cut of meat or a new car, regardless of how expensive they may be. For some, it is being able to go to an exclusive, trendy and expensive restaurant, but for others it may simply be being able to go out to eat at all.

Briefly, luxury is something rare and hedonic, difficult to acquire or use, that provides the perception of unique experiences in combination with enhancement or reinforcement of the social position. In short, it is an emotional social marker and differentiator. Contrasting common beliefs, we suggest that luxury goods satisfy needs of people.

Our goal is to present the essence of what is behind luxury. In the following chapters we will reveal its "hidden" aspects, it's drivers and tools to manage luxury in a more profitable and sustainable way.

Driven by the finding that hypothetically all categories could have a luxury tier, and the conclusion that many luxury brands are not managed appropriately, managers of luxury brands will profit from a hands-on how to do guide centered around six winning strategies of luxury management. And managers of non-luxury brands will profit as well as the book provides insights on how the most desirable items are marketed. This provides great opportunities for innovation, more relevant and more successful products.

Daniel A. Langer & Oliver P. Heil, January 2015

Chapter 1: What is Luxury?

Objective:
Provide a solid point of departure in understanding luxury

Key aspects:
- Luxury is not always defined with sharp precision
- The term "luxury" is often used too "casually"
- Luxuries should be able to send a clear "signal"
- Key aspects include exclusivity, uniqueness, scarcity, and heritage
- Luxuries typically enhance or reinforce social status
- A segmentation of luxury consumers is introduced
- Luxury goods may provide unique experiences

What are luxury products all about? What is the distinction versus a "normal" product? Why are consumers buying luxury products and why are they willing to accept the related price premiums? How does the consumption situation or context influence the product's perception? How can this perception be steered profitably? In short: what is the formula of luxury?

In this book we strive to answer this question proposing a comprehensive approach to luxury and guidance for managers how to manage luxury goods.

There is something ambiguous about luxury: Naturally, it seems to be part of the lifestyle of the rich, and it seems to be desired and longed for by most. Despite being part of the dreams of a lot of people however, luxury is often discussed controversially in private as in public. It therefore seems to be both, desired as well as condemned.

Two of the typical attributes of luxury, "expensive" and "exclusive", suggest that luxury is rare, and yet the term can be found in an almost ubiquitous way in products, services and articles. Google (Jul 24, 2012) gave a whopping 799 million hits for the term "luxury", much more than for example for "bread" (ca. 359 million), an item one would typically consider as non-luxury.

This ubiquity of the luxury term and its usage in different contexts suggests that many people, including consumers and marketers, may not always use "luxury" in a unique and precise meaning. As a result, researchers may also use the term too casually, evidence that we found reviewing the luxury-related papers. We conclude that a specific definition of luxury is needed in order to extract precise strategies for its management. A precise definition of luxury and full understanding of its determinants will allow steering of luxury brands more precisely and more profitably.

As point of departure, luxury consumption could be described as a socially discriminating consumption, which offers a way to position oneself uniquely within the social landscape (see Figure 1).

This has two consequences: First, a luxury should be able to send a very clear signal towards people, so that there is a minimization of any confusion between a luxury and a non-luxury. Second, exclusivity is key. Luxury is rather unique, difficult – in acquiring or use –, scarce, conspicuous and connected with a heritage: it's, in a sense, me = yes, others = no.

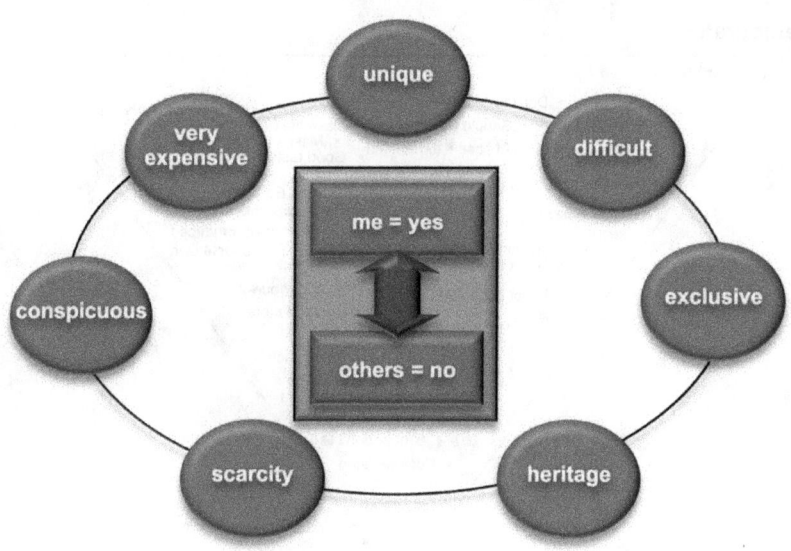

Figure 1: Point of Departure – Luxury Aspects

So how do people's view on luxury differ? Dubois et al. (2005) suggest several segments of consumers based on their attitudes toward luxury (see Figure 2). First, they describe "elitists", who believe that luxury is for few people only. Some attributes those connect with luxury are "good taste", "refined people", "could talk for hours", "make life beautiful", "makes dream" and "education needed".

Members of the second segment – the "democrats" – perceive luxury as less exclusive and in a rather omnipresent way. According to them, luxury "is not reserved for 'refined' people, and no special education is needed to fully appreciate it. Luxury is neither synonymous with a narrow and selective idea of 'good taste' nor an instrument of differentiation from others. It is not necessarily very expensive" (Dubois et al. 2005, p.121).

Democratic   **Elitist**

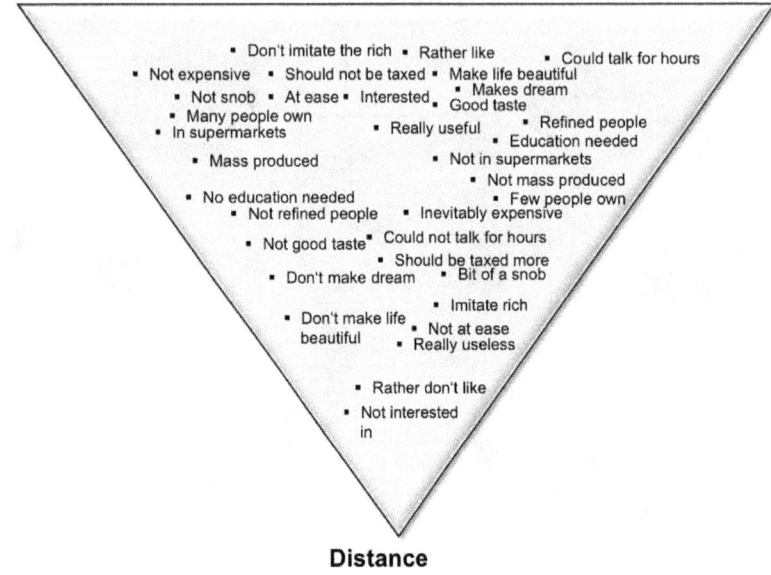

- Don't imitate the rich • Rather like   • Could talk for hours
• Not expensive • Should not be taxed • Make life beautiful
  • Not snob • At ease • Interested • Makes dream
                                                            • Good taste
  • Many people own   • Really useful   • Refined people
  • In supermarkets   • Education needed
    • Mass produced   • Not in supermarkets
                                                          • Not mass produced
  • No education needed   • Few people own
    • Not refined people • Inevitably expensive
      • Not good taste • Could not talk for hours
                          • Should be taxed more
    • Don't make dream   • Bit of a snob
                                • Imitate rich
      • Don't make life • Not at ease
        beautiful   • Really useless

      • Rather don't like
      • Not interested
      in

Distance

Figure 2: Consumer Segments: Attitudes Towards Luxury
Source: Dubois et al. 2005, p.123

Third, they identify "distant" consumers who "believe that luxury is a different world to which they do not belong" (Dubois et al. 2005, p.122). Distant consumers state to be less attracted by luxury. They see luxury rather negatively, as useless or too expensive. They do not believe much in superior quality of luxury and state to be content with a fine replica rather than the original. On top, they do not feel at ease in a luxury surrounding like a luxury shop. Luxury is not at all perceived as being part of their lifestyle.

However, even if some people feel distant or reject luxury, there seems to be a "need" for luxury products, given that luxury products are a means of differentiation and of extending the own personality. Thus, along Maslow's need hierarchy from survival towards self-actualization, luxury should play – in general – an important role in people's lives (see Kemp 1998).

More particularly, any product that is able to improve one's own social position within a social reference group should be – at least on a subconscious level – an important product for any person, independent of own rational assessments.

We therefore suggest that luxury is important for most people – if not for all – independent of the individual rational evaluation. Nevertheless, the rational evaluation – reflected in the segmentation of elitists, democrats and distant consumers – would most likely influence purchase planning, purchase behavior and purchase explanation to oneself and others.

Without doubt, price and income play an important role for luxury. It is a common view that income elasticity of luxury should be above 1 (e.g. Dubois and Duquesne 1993, Encyclopaedia Britannica 2006). This is also suggested by simple logic: a higher available budget leads to a higher likelihood of buying a product at the top end of a product range.

But luxury clearly emerges beyond price. Many authors highlighted that the experiences (past and expected) triggered by a luxury product are important drivers. The importance of the luxury experience correlates with the description of Friedman (2007, online) on elements that luxury consumers seek. They incorporate surprise, charm, desire, and allure: "...what constitutes luxury becomes a wholly individual and emotional decision. It becomes about what people don't know."

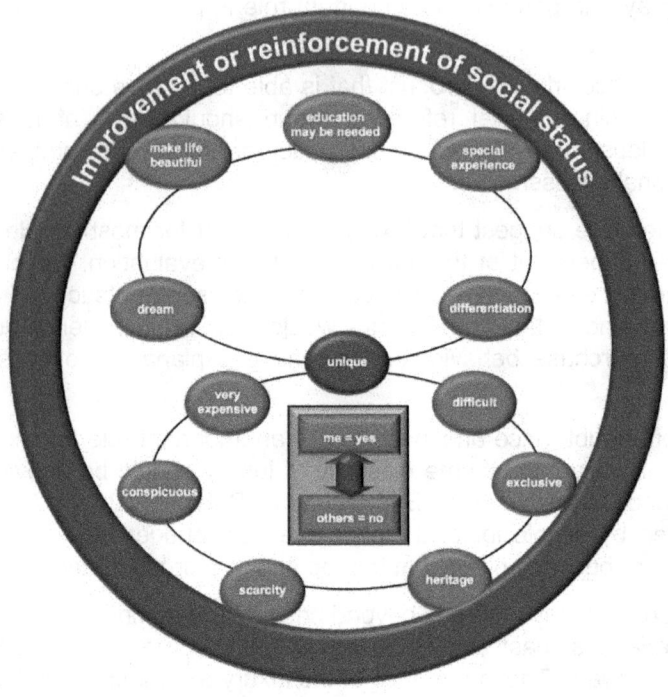

Figure 3: Luxury Aspects (Extended)

Also, luxuries might require special education as Dubois et al. (2005) indicate when looking at elitists. This aspect may increase the perception of socially differentiating consumption.

As a result, luxury's function as social differentiator in combination with unique experiences can make luxury products and brand relevant and desired even for people who consciously show distance to luxury consumption. The aspects play a key role in why people consume luxuries.

Belk's (1985, 1988) research underlines that products and their possessions and consumption play an important role for people, functioning as an extended self. If a possession is lost or even stolen,

22

people also lose part of their identity and memories. This explains why many people develop a strong emotional relationship to some valuable items they own.

Belk proposes that materialism changes over lifespan in terms of a shift of purely accumulating or consuming products towards accumulating experiences, another indicator of the importance of experiences.

There is a negative externality connected with many luxury items: the more people own or use a luxury good, the less value it holds. Understanding this is a key success factor in managing luxury. Thus, the degree of self-extension by luxury goods is, in a sense, a **function of exclusivity**.

As we could see, just being expensive or differentiating is not describing a luxury with enough precision. A luxury is rather a bundle of aspects that make it exclusive and unique in comparison to a non-luxury. While pleasure, abundance and indulgence are typically related to luxury, we suggest more specifically that luxuries provide exceptionally unique experiences in combination with an improvement or reinforcement of the social position. The uniqueness of a luxury is further a result of being a dream, its perceived ability to make life more beautiful, and its ability to differentiate.

Chapter 2: Luxury Categories and Luxury Index

Objective:
Provide an innovative tool to assess the potential of luxury categories

Key aspects:
- Assessment of most luxurious categories with new "luxury index"
- Category assessment allows a more profitable management of brands
- Precise identification of portfolio opportunities
- Assessment of how consistent brands are managed across categories
- Benchmark categories against others to distill luxury opportunities
- Innovation management: create new, more luxurious offers
- High practicability: easy-to-use, hands-on tool

Why is this important to understand the category potential of luxury? For a company that is already operating in the luxury tier, a category potential analysis offers the chance to benchmark the served categories against other categories. As a result of such benchmarking, potentials for new, even more exclusive and luxurious offers that allow higher premiums and profits may be identified.

Also the relative position towards competitors within the category and across categories can be identified in order to optimize and harmonize the company's price positioning. In terms of portfolio, the category potential assessment may additionally serve to identify the ability to win if a company expands to other categories.

The category potential analysis also helps to identify the attractiveness to operate in a luxury category in terms of its development stage and of its competitiveness. If a category has not yet developed a luxury tier, the first mover might have an advantage by "owning" the top tier. On the other hand, the development of a category towards a luxury category may also be difficult, costly and risky, as consumer perceptions need to be changed.

How can the category potential be assessed? Central assumption is that theoretically all categories could have a top tier that is perceived as luxury tier. This may lead to two possible assessment results for a category: there already exists a luxury tier or there is not yet a luxury tier developed.

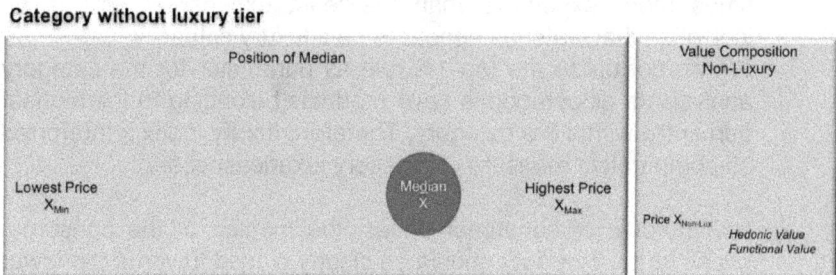

Figure 4: Luxury Category Assessment Parameters

As parameters for an assessment of the luxury potential of a category, we propose the differential between highest and lowest price as well as the median of prices. Limiting the criteria to price information has the advantage to be able to compare several categories quantitatively independent of their nature. There may be other criteria including subjective assessments. However, we propose the price-related approach due to being simple, transparent, fast and independent of individual views.

Figure 4 visualizes our proposition of a price-related luxury category assessment. We assume a category to be a luxury category if two of the following observations can be made at the same time:

- High absolute price differential – can be several hundred thousand or even several million Euros depending on the category – between the least expensive and the most expensive product. We suggest measuring and comparing the differential with a "luxury index" that divides the highest price by the lowest price of a category. In case of luxury we expect the price of the most expensive product to be a sizeable multiple of the least expensive product's price. Rationale is the scope of the added luxury value.

  A good example is the watch category (see Table 2). While a cheap watch can be bought starting from $5, the most expensive watch has a price tag of $1.6 million, resulting in an index of 320,000. The most expensive item of the category is 320,000 times more expensive than the least expensive. This is an indication that watches appear to be a luxury category.

  We do not utilize the top 1% rule as parameter for the category analysis as all categories have products belonging to the highest percentile within the category. Therefore luxury index is preferred as comparative measure of category luxuriousness.

- Low median of consumer prices: the median of the consumer prices of the category should be clearly biased towards the lower end of prices within a category if the category has a luxury tier. Again, the rationale is the significant added luxury value of the top category products, which indicate that the top end should be far away from the middle of the market. If a category lacks a luxury tier, prices should be rather close and the median should be rather located in the middle of the price range or biased towards the price of the more expensive products. In the watch category, we estimate the median of prices at approximately $200. This is at the absolute low end of the interval of prices in the category: a second clear indicator for the luxuriousness of the watch category.

To apply the logic and generate findings we analyzed fifty categories, of which half are "durable" categories (e.g. flat-screen TV, car) and half are "non-durable" categories or services (e.g. laundry detergent, spa treatment). The analysis was done utilizing our best estimate on lowest, median and highest price point per category.

The price information was based on extensive store-checks in Germany, France and Spain as well as internet research between October 2007 and December 2010.

The categories have been subjectively chosen, however we intended to cover popular and common categories (e.g. car, laptop, house, shampoo, face cream, toothpaste) as well as some categories, which are often referred to as luxury categories (e.g. champagne, spa treatment, set of golf-clubs, yacht charter).

The findings are shown in Table 2, with an indication of the prices X_{Min}, X_{Max} and $\overline{X}$. The position of the median within the category is shown as percentage value, resulting of the equation:

$$\frac{\overline{X}-X_{Min}}{X_{Max}-X_{Min}}*100.$$

The percentage indicates the position of the median in the price interval $[X_{Min}; X_{Max}]$. If the median is close to the lowest price of the category, the indicator will be close to 0%. If the median is close to the highest price, the indicator will be close to 100%. We visualize the percentage utilizing a red dot on a line that represents the scale from 0 to 100.

The last column shows the luxury index, dividing X_{Max} by X_{Min}. The index shows how many times the highest category price can be divided by the lowest, somehow indicating the scope of added luxury value in a category. As a starting point, we have three main observations:

- Both groups, durables and non-durables, show a wide spread of the total value of the luxury index, which suggests that luxuriousness is not necessarily dependent of being a durable good or a commodity or service. This outcome is consistent with the proposition that all categories may have a luxury tier.

— Comparing absolute prices of both groups however indicates that the willingness-to-pay seems to have the tendency to be higher for durables compared to non-durables. This is consistent with the findings on higher requirements towards the durability of luxury that we indicated. In a sense, durability facilitates luxury and drives the willingness-to-pay. On the other hand, also non-durable goods are seen and purchased as luxuries with significant premiums.

— The five observed categories with the highest luxury index are:

I: Lingerie, index 5,000,000 with the most expensive offer at $15,000,000.

II. Cell-phones, index 1,300,000, most expensive offer at $1,300,000.

III. Shoes for women, index 400,000, most expensive offer at $2,000,000.

IV. Watches, index 320,000, most expensive offer at $1,600,000.

V. Wine, index 160,000, most expensive offer at $160,000.

Those five categories additionally have a median position of 0% within the price interval, thus they are clear luxury categories according to the defined criteria. Being the most luxurious among the observed categories, it is interesting to have a closer look at their top item in order to distill managerial implications.

The highest price tag for lingerie belongs to Victoria's Secret's Red Hot Fantasy combo, which Giselle Bundchen was wearing during the opening of the Victoria's Secret flagship store on New York's Broadway. The set is made of 1,300 stones that include 300 carats of Thai rubies surrounded by sprays of diamonds. Only one was ever made, and due to its value and uniqueness, the purchase price includes delivery in an armored van with specially trained security guards. The combo has not been sold yet, although it attracted numerous enquiries since its appearance in the Victoria's Secret's catalogue (Sussman 2005).

The value of the item is a result of absolute uniqueness composed by being one item only, being worn by one of the world's most bespoken top-models at a unique flagship-store opening event, being delivered in a unique way, combined with unique craftsmanship utilizing rare materials. The premium of consumption makes it even more valuable: If it were ever worn, the wearer needed probably a special diet regime or even a plastic surgery to be able to match the measures of Giselle Bundchen and high security measures are needed for storage and usage. In a nutshell, the item is all about uniqueness in an extreme way, requiring high premiums of consumption and ownership.

The most expensive cell-phone is the Ancord Diamond Crypto Smartphone, made by Australian designer Peter Aloisson. The phone is made of solid platinum 950, logo and navigation key are made of 18 carat yellow gold. Each side of the phone features 25 1/2 carat princess diamonds. The website describes uniqueness as key value driver: "Status is expressed in everyday objects. A cell phone by Peter Aloisson makes the difference. It is pure indulgence for those who want the very best. Every piece is a one-of-a-kind creation among millions of cell phones. This is what makes them special, with such unique items you can stand out and display your individuality. In unique and exclusive designs that use radiance and glamour to bring attention to their owners and to the pieces themselves" (Aloisson 2007, online).

Similar to the most expensive lingerie, the most expensive shoes, the $2 million Stuart Weizman 2004 "Cinderella slippers", feature more than five hundred diamonds on a platinum frame, including one rare cognac-colored 5 carat diamond, worth $1 million alone, and were worn by Oscar-nominated singer Alison Kraus at the 2004 Oscars ceremony (Stuart Weizman 2007). The combination of craftsmanship, materials and a unique legend ("worn at the Oscars") drive the value.

The most expensive watch, the $1.6 million Vacheron Constantin Tour de L'Ile, has been already discussed. More than 10,000 man-hours that are needed to build the watch by the world's best watchmakers make the Tour de L'Ile absolutely unique in terms of craftsmanship. The watch was built in a limited edition of only 7 pieces for the 250th anniversary of Vacheron Constantin.

The 1787 Chateau Lafitte (it is now spelled Lafite) is the most expensive wine, sold at Christie's in London in December 1985 for $160,000. Patrick Radden Keefe (2007, online) explains in the New Yorker: "...evidence suggested that the wine had belonged to Thomas Jefferson, and that the bottle at auction could 'rightly be considered one of the world's greatest rarities.' The level of the wine was 'exceptionally high' for such an old bottle — just half an inch below the cork — and the color 'remarkably deep for its age.' The wine's value was listed as 'inestimable.'" Jefferson spent today's equivalent of $125,000 on wine during his first presidential term and is regarded as America's first wine connoisseur, a passion that he developed during his term as America's Minister to France before his presidency. The bottle has one absolute unique feature: the initials "Th.J." printed on the glass. According to Passmore (2003, online), those initials are "what ensured the record price tag…"

The wine was not bought to be drunk as 200 years is beyond any limit for wines. Passmore (2003, online) concludes: "The allure of these high-priced bottles of vinegar, and other wines of its ilk, is purely in the joy of collecting, not consuming. The 1787 Lafite was explicitly bought as a piece of Jefferson memorabilia, not as a bottle of wine, and it now resides in the Forbes Collection in New York." Also in this case there is a unique combination of craftsmanship, limited availability and a legend.

Table 2: Luxury Potential Analysis

Category		Lowest[E] Price X_{Min}	Highest[E] Price X_{Max}	Median[E] X	Position of Median X within Category	Index X_{Max} : X_{Min}
	Flat Screen TV	€250	€100,000	€1,200	1.0%	400
	Car	€7,500	€1,660,000	€28,000	1.2%	221
	House	$30,000	$1bn	$200,000	0.0%	33,333
	Watch	$5	$1,600,000	€200	0.0%	320,000
	Home telephone	€15	€880	€50	4.0%	59
	Cell phone	€1 (with contract)	€1,300,000	€100	0.0%	1,300,000
	Handbag	€9	€261,000	€60	0.0%	29,000
	Stereo speakers	$20	$1,000,000	$150	0.0%	50,000
	Audio cable (3,6m)	$2	$7,250	$10	0.1%	3,625
	Headphones	$5	$15,900	$40	0.2%	3,180
	Laptop	$133	$1,000,000	$1,300	0.1%	7,519
	Mouse pad	$2	$500	$8	1.2%	250
	Shoes (men)	$5	$1,830	$80	4.1%	366
	Shoes (women)	$5	$2,000,000	$80	0.0%	400,000
	Lingerie	$3	$15,000,000	$35	0.0%	5,000,000
	Jeans	$15	$10,000	$70	0.6%	667
	Men's suit (off the rack)	$60	$15,000	$300	1.6%	250
	Teddy bear	$9	$84,000	$20	0.0%	9,333
	Bathroom faucet	$20	$4,500	$60	0.9%	225
	Set of golf clubs	$179	$32,000	$300	0.4%	179
	Bed	$89	$1,600,000	$300	0.0%	17,978
Durable Goods	Vacuum cleaner	$9.99	$1,800	$100	4.5%	180
	Pencil	$0.20	$9,500	$2	0.0%	47,500
	Fountain Pen	$9	$730,000	$50	0.0%	81,111
	Electric Shaver	€5	€350	€125	36.2%	70

	Category	Lowest[E] Price X_{Min}	Highest[E] Price X_{Max}	Median[E] X	Position of Median X within Category	Index X_{Max} : X_{Min}
Non-Durable Goods and Services	Omelet	$2	$1,000	$8	0.6%	500
	Dinner meal (15 people)	$100	$30,000	$200	0.3%	300
	Desert	$2	$14,500	$8	0.0%	7,250
	Chocolate (500g)	$1.80	$2,600	$4	0.1%	1,440
	Ice-cream (Scoop)	$0.40	$200	$1	0.3%	500
	Caffè latte	$0.70	$20	$2.50	9.3%	29
	Hotel suite (1 night)	$130	$30,000	$280	0.5%	231
	Cigarettes	$3	$100,000	$3.50	0.0%	33,333
	Water (750ml)	$0.30	$60	$0.60	0.5%	200
	Wine (bottle)	$1	$160,000	$8.50	0.0%	160,000
	Beer (bottle)	$0.30	$100	$0.60	0.3%	333
	Milk (1l)	$0.50	$45	$0.80	1.7%	90
	Apple juice (1000 ml)	$0.90	$14	$1.25	2.7%	16
	Yacht charter (week)	€500	€660,000	€6,000	0.8%	1,320
	Spa treatment	$40	$5,000	$75	0.7%	125
	Whisky (bottle)	$12	$38,000	$30	0.0%	3,167
	Cognac (0.75l bottle)	€16	€200,000	€40	0.0%	12,500
	Champagne (0.75l bottle)	€13	€750	€25	1.6%	58
	Toilet paper	$0.20	$30	$0.35	0.5%	150
	Laundry Detergent (1kg)	€1.66	€6	€3.00	50%	3.6
	Perfume	$2	$215,000	$30	0.0%	107,500
	Toothpaste	$1.20	$15	$1.80	4.3%	12,5
	Face Cream (150ml)	$1.20	$2,645	$10	0.2%	2,204
	Shampoo (200ml)	€0.50	€100	€2	1.5%	200
	Airline ticket Frankfurt-NYC	€385	€6,900	€550	2.5%	18

[E] Best estimate based on store checks, internet research (e.g. forbes.com, forbestraveller.com, pricerunner.com, most-expensive.net), Oct 2007–Dec 2010

What do those top-items have in common?

- An absolute price typically above $1 million (exception of wine), making them affordable for a small segment only.
- An index >100,000 between cheapest and most expensive item of the category, clearly setting the top item apart from the rest.
- Strict limitation of the number of available items. In the case of wine and lingerie it is one piece only, in the other cases it is a handful of pieces.
- A legend in form of a unique story connected to the items, which increases the exclusivity in addition to the limited availability.
- They are rather "pieces of art", bought to be collected, and they are normally not everyday objects.
- They are a result of exceptional craftsmanship, handmade and handpicked.

With an assessment that is based on few conveniently searchable price-related parameters we propose a way to benchmark the luxury potential of different categories. We suggest that benchmarking is an important starting point in strategy development for luxury. The category benchmarking can be further detailed to brand or product level.

Already on a category level clear differences become evident. Looking at the top, categories like lingerie, cell-phones, women's shoes, watches, wines, perfumes, cigarettes, fountain pens or handbags are rather different in their nature and have no evident connection. Other categories, often attributed to luxury, such as champagne, cars, first class travel, spa treatments, or dinner meals are positioned somewhat in the middle and have strong further luxury potential. Some other categories, such as electric shavers clearly lack a luxury tier that can be called "developed" at this point in time.

It underlines the proposition that theoretically all categories can become luxury categories and it additionally shows that a luxury tier must be actively developed to unleash and exploit the full potential: The more a product or brand is able to develop a unique proposition, in its extreme reduced to one absolutely unique item, more a piece of art than a product, the more added luxury value is created and the more expensive the items may become.

The similar price tag for the most expensive bed, car and cell-phone, being exceeded by factor 10 by the most expensive lingerie, underlines that the prices for luxury goods are strongly disconnected from the functional value and composed to a large extent by added luxury value from uniqueness of the item and the ability to differentiate from others.

In terms of strategy, a category analysis may lead to the following considerations for a company willing to serve the luxury segment:

- Which is the right category to focus?
- Where is the ability to win: developing the luxury tier and extending the luxuriousness of the category (category growth and value creation), competing within the existing luxury tier (value creation), competing below the existing luxury (price competition compared to the top offer).
- Is the own portfolio consistent across categories, hence is the relative price compared with the top offer in the market consistent across categories, leading to a consistent brand positioning?
- Which are unfulfilled consumer insights that can be leveraged?
- Which are relevant legends and stories that add uniqueness?
- Which are the "rules" of the luxury tier in terms of positioning the brand?
- How can a luxury brand be further differentiated and individualized in order to boost added luxury value?

In sum, the assessment helps to define profitable and sustainable strategies for luxury brands and products. On top, the luxury index combined with the position of own products within the price interval of the served categories may be utilized as key performance indicator to benchmark the performance of a luxury brand.

Chapter 3: The Hidden Aspects of Luxury

> **Objective:**
> Provide key concepts of luxury
>
> **Key aspects:**
> - "Hidden Aspects" of luxury
> - Comprehensive overview of luxury propositions
> - Added Luxury Value (ALV)
> - Individual perception of luxury
> - Luxury Signaling

Let's examine more closely what luxury is all about. So far we saw that luxury has got to be expensive, exclusive, scarce, and maybe conspicuous. It is unique because it is often a dream. It makes life more beautiful. It provides a special experience and can be a source of sensual pleasure. Education may sometimes be needed to fully appreciate the luxury. And it is a means to differentiate from others, reinforcing or improving the social position.

However, even if all these attributes can be applied for a luxury good, we believe that it is still not sufficient to describe and explain luxury as a whole. Instead, we are looking for further aspects that allow a more distinct and precise separation of a luxury from a non-luxury. We are looking to decode the "hidden" aspects of luxury.

This indicates that there must be something more about luxury, further aspects that truly separate luxury from non-luxury. Those separators would be luxury aspects that should be able to explain the true "magic" of luxury and, thus, enable to manage luxury more efficiently. In our extended frame in Figure 5 we indicate these aspects with a question mark for the time being.

Our aim is to decode these distinct and so far rather "hidden" aspects of luxury and to come up with a sharper operational definition. To do so, we will build clusters of its several facets, which we condense into several dimensions and further into propositions for luxury (see Table 3 for an overview, Langer & Heil 2013 for more detail).

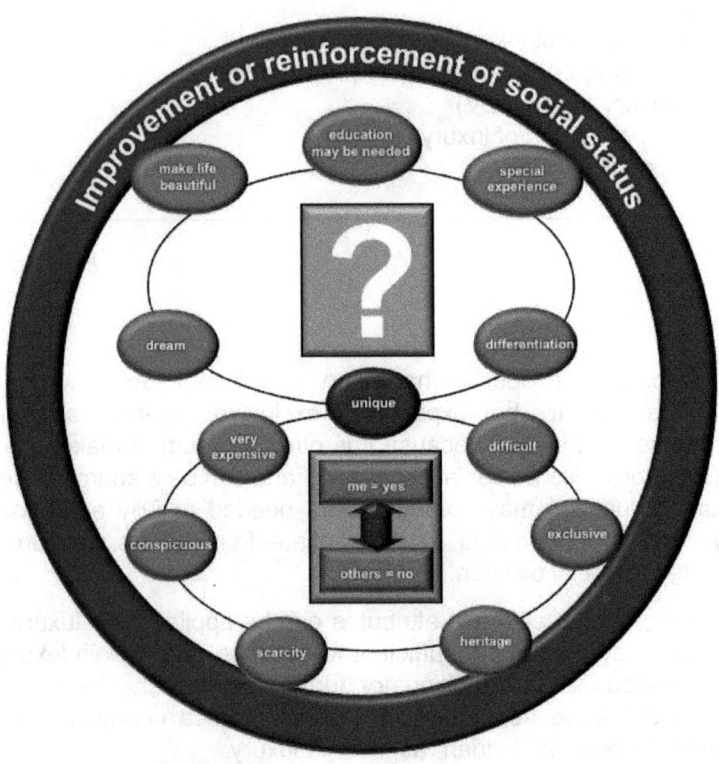

Figure 5: Known and Hidden Luxury Aspects

Table 3: Overview of Luxury Propositions

Dimension	Proposition	
Distinction	P1	Luxury has distinctive, exclusive items or values, different from non-luxury goods.
Importance & Added Value	P2.1	Luxury is of very high importance for the purchaser and consumer.
	P2.2	Luxury goods provide a significant added luxury value ALV compared to non-luxuries.
Individual Perception	P3	The individual purchasing power and the accumulated purchase and consumption experiences influence the individual perception of a good being luxury or not.
Luxury Signaling	P4.1	Luxury goods transmit a signal with status information that is attributed to the owner or consumer.
	P4.2	The clearer and less distorted the luxury signal becomes, the better a luxury good can define status.
	P4.3	The stronger the luxury signal becomes, the better a luxury good can define status (in case of a clear signal).
	P4.4	The more consistent luxury signals become, the better a luxury good can define status.
	P4.5	The more a luxury good is perceived as "showing-off", the less it can define status.
	P4.6	With a more consistent luxury signal the tendency towards discreet luxury consumption increases.
	P4.7	There is a positive correlation between the luxury signal of attributing status information and added luxury value.
	P4.8	Both, the owner and others (e.g. is peers) can receive and process luxury signals.
	P4.9	Luxury signal perception depends on preconditions of the receptor as well as the "offensiveness" of the category.
Intrinsic and Extrinsic Functions	P5.1	Luxury goods enable a mind-set change towards new experiences by allowing living and realizing dreams.
	P5.2	Luxury adds self-esteem.
	P5.3	Luxury adds "aura" of being a connoisseur and expert.
	P5.4	Luxury signals financial liquidity and economic power.
	P5.5	Luxury signals social dominance.
	P5.6	Luxury as head-turner, enhancing attractiveness and looks: "makes ugly people look better".
	P5.7	Luxury enhances self-perception
	P5.8	Luxury as ultimate protector and social shelter: "no other has a better product."
	P5.9	Luxury enhances the perceived decision-quality or decision-expertise.

Dimension	Proposition	
	P5.10	Luxury signals hedonic aspects like enjoyment, fun, pleasure and unique experiences: it is "the ultimate treat".
Group Marker, "ID Code"	P6.1	Luxury goods function as group markers, attributing the membership to certain social groups.
	P6.2	Luxury can have the function of the minimum expected product within a social group.
Luxury Categories & Position	P7.1	Hypothetically, luxury goods can be found in every product category.
	P7.2	Assuming normal distribution of prices within a category, we propose that generally the top 1% of all goods along the price dimension have the potential to be luxury goods.

Added Luxury Value

We assume that a good can be categorized either as luxury or as non-luxury. It means that there are distinctive items or values separating luxury from the rest, and distinct product clusters

This implies that people can differentiate a luxury from a non-luxury due to specific properties or what they perceive as added value. A common belief is that a luxury good is typically not a necessity. In her article in Financial Times about what luxury means now, Friedmann (2007, online) even goes as far as stating that luxury "…is never necessary." A typical rationale is that the functional benefits of a luxury can normally be achieved with other, non-luxury goods.

Nevertheless, the "non-essential" facet of luxury has two limitations. First, if the perceived value of a luxury product leads to price premiums that are clearly above any essential product and that are clearly understood in a common sense as "luxury price", can we then speak of something non-essential? Why would someone pay a luxury premium for something without a major importance to his or her life?

Secondly, where is the borderline? Where does an indispensable minimum end – hence, the essential good? Where does the "essential" end and the "luxury" start?

We conclude that being non-essential, extravagant or (over-)indulging is not a decisive separator for the luxury category. Luxury might be non-essential in terms of its pure functional values: A $20 radio also produces a sound and would therefore deliver similar functional values compared to a high-end sound system. However, the fact that people are willing to pay significant premiums for luxuries clearly indicates that it should indeed be of very high importance for the purchaser and consumer.

According to our point of view, luxuries are those few goods that are able to provide a "significant additional value" versus a normal and even a premium good. In line with economic theory, this additional luxury value justifies the significant price premium typically associated with luxury.

In other words, if we look into each product category, luxury products should be at the top end in terms of pricing. Given the connection of price and perceived value, the significant price premiums of luxury need to be coherent with a significant added value provided by the luxury (see Simonson and Drolet 2004 for an in-depth assessment on willingness-to-pay).

We suggest naming the significant additional value that luxuries provide as "added luxury value" or "ALV".

Added luxury value ALV is the extraordinary value beyond any functional value and even beyond the additional emotional or hedonic value of a premium product. We suggest that added luxury value is created by distinct intrinsic and extrinsic functions of luxuries, thus functions that affect the owner or consumer and functions that affect others.

We further suggest that added luxury value is able to exceed the functional and emotional value of a good by far. Our rationale is the huge difference in price between normal or premium goods and luxury goods within a category. Let's have a look at cars and let's assume the "normal" pricing range at about $10,000 to $30,000, the "premium" range at about $30,000 to $100,000, and the luxury range above with products including some exceeding $1,000,000 like the Bugatti Veyron. It becomes obvious that the huge deltas even between the top premium offers and some luxury offers may be multiples of the premium prices.

Consumers will only pay for those deltas if the total perceived value of the luxury matches or exceeds the luxury price, composed by functional, emotional and added luxury value (see Figure 6). Subsequently, we will explore how a luxury is able to create and provide the added luxury value. We will also distill of which elements the added luxury value is composed.

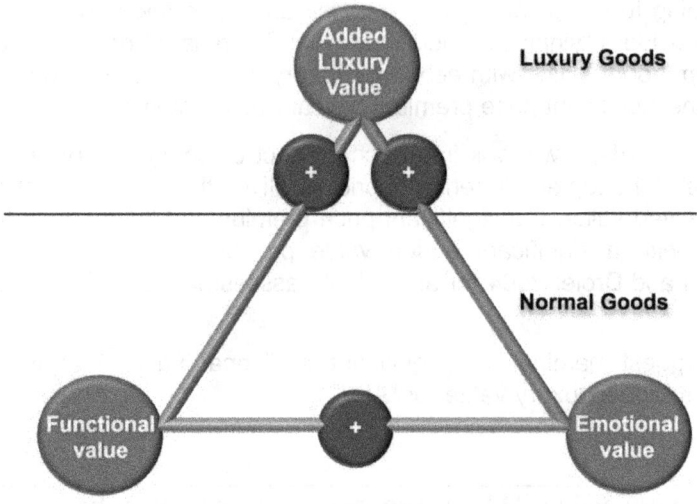

Figure 6: Added Luxury Value ALV

Individual Perception of Luxury

Both, the importance of luxury for the individual person and its added value, explain the definition of luxury by Wikipedia (2008, online): Luxury is seen as "a good for which demand increases more than proportionally as income rises, contrast with inferior good and normal good… It must be noted, though, that income elasticity of demand is not constant with respect to income, and may change sign at different levels of income."

It means that a luxury good may become a normal good or even an inferior good at different income or wealth levels. For example a wealthy person may stop buying increasing numbers of luxury cars for his or her automobile collection to start collecting airplanes or yachts, while the latter examples may apply to very few people only.

This adds two additional facets to the definition of luxury: first, individual income or wealth, hence the individual purchasing power. Second, as a result, the same product can be both, luxury or non-luxury, depending on the viewpoint of the consumer (see also Kemp 1998).

> **The perception of a good being luxury or not therefore also seems to differ depending on the individual purchase and consumption history, hence the accumulated experiences. It is expected to change over time at different wealth levels.**

It suggests an individual demand curve for a specific luxury good that is not always increasing with increasing income, but decreasing again from a certain income level (Langer & Heil 2013).

Luxury Signaling

One of the most interesting aspects of the luxury definition is the question: what makes people buy or consume luxuries? We already extracted one key aspect: the significant added value ALV. It makes the purchase of a luxury good important for an individual, thus justifying significant luxury price premiums. We will therefore need to understand how ALV is perceived and created to fully understand and describe luxury.

The point of departure to conceptualize the added luxury value is the assumption that a luxury good is sending signals about the social status of owner or consumer, Luxuries would therefore have the function to rank people by the status information signal (Rationale and further reading in Langer & Heil 2013).

We propose that this connection can be explained by a signal that attributes status information to the owner or consumer. We suggest that "luxury signaling" is one of the fundamental concepts in explaining luxury.

We suggest that three important dimensions influence the perception of the luxury signal: signal clarity, signal strength and consistency of signals (see Figure 7).

The clarity or purity of the luxury signal describes whether it can be perceived clearly or whether it is distorted by inconsistencies, incongruent information or attributes that do not fit. For example a Rolex that would be sold at a discount price, let's assume for $100, would have an unclear signal. Some attributes of the watch, like craftsmanship, design, heritage and experience, might remain undistorted and clear. The price would not fit anymore to the luxury product's expectation and positioning, hence the signal would become somewhat fuzzy, at least to a person who knows about the distorted element.

For others, however, who do not know that the price does not fit to the luxury good, the product would still be perceived as luxury. This explains the popularity of fake "luxury" watches or fake "luxury" handbags, which transmit – in case the fake is not recognized as such – a luxury signal towards others.

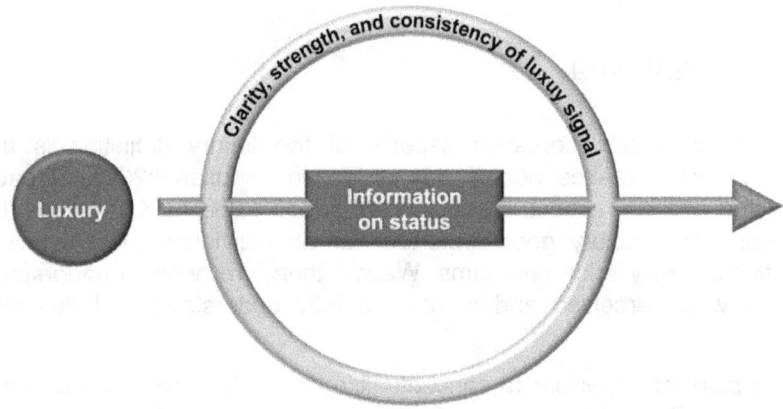

Figure 7: Dimensions of Luxury Signaling

We suggest that signal clarity is decisive to perceive the luxury signal: the clearer the signal is, the better the product can attribute status information. The better status information can be attributed, the better a product can be classified and perceived as "luxury" from a consumer perspective.

The strength of the luxury signal is connected to the awareness about the luxury good or its items. The stronger the signal is, and assuming the signal is clear, the more status information will be attributed. However, if the signal is distorted and strong, it will accelerate the negative perception.

In the most extreme case it means that a product that is not known at all, hence a product or brand without any awareness even in the luxury target group, will hardly be perceived as a luxury. The higher the brand awareness and equity (e.g. by brand names, designs and experiences), the more a clear signal can define status.

As third influencing parameter on the luxury signal we identify consistency of signals. While the two first parameters are directly linked to a distinct luxury good, the consistency of signals is a result of all product-related perceptions about a person.

Consistency of signals therefore depends on the person or sender. If a person predominantly uses luxury products, the signals of those products are suggested to be consistent. We further suggest that consistent signals can be perceived and processed easier. As a result, the more consistent a person is in terms of luxury ownership and consumption, the better the related luxury goods are able to attribute status information. This is due to easier signal perception.

We also suggest the existence of a perceived "expertise" in consuming luxury, especially when luxury consumption becomes more consistent. If someone is very rich, owns a lot of luxury goods and permanently "shows-off" in a very visible way, others might perceive this as the behavior of someone not educated enough to consume luxury: "luxury expertise" is missing. People typically refer to this phenomenon claiming, "This person is truly a show-off". Thus, there is a risk that showing-off luxury in a too flashy way even decreases the perceived status.

An outcome of the previous findings is that owning and consuming luxury may require a balance between showing and not showing. This balance is an important precondition to achieve the anticipated result of enhancing or improving the social status. In a sense, the sender can become a moderator of the luxury signal. This underlines once more the expected tendency towards a more discreet consumption of luxury with increased level of luxury consumption. Once the luxury signal becomes more consistent and easier to perceive, luxury consumption may become more discreet.

The latter proposition reveals a dilemma in consuming luxury: a certain visibility and consistency is needed to stimulate signal perception by others and enhance status. Too much visibility, on the other hand, counters the intended effect, and might decrease the status perception.

We suggested before that signaling of status information is a key concept of understanding, defining and managing luxury: it is the fundamental base of how consumers perceive added luxury value. We suggest that the clearer, stronger and more consistent status information is signaled and attributed, the stronger added luxury value is perceived.

In a nutshell, added luxury value can be described as follows:

Added Luxury Value: The significant added value of a luxury good is the ability of a good to improve or reinforce the individual situation within the social context.

It explains in part why people desire and buy luxuries and why they pay significant premiums: they are willing to pay the luxury premium in exchange for the added luxury value. The perception of ALV depends on the signal. As a consequence, the clearer, stronger and more consistent the signal, the higher the willingness to pay luxury premiums should become.

It is furthermore important that not only the peers or other people receive and process the luxury signal. Additionally, the person who owns or consumes the luxury becomes a signal receptor and processor. This is consistent with Belk (1988), who classifies possessions as personality drivers.

Both, the owner and others (e.g. his peers) can receive and process luxury signals.

Hence, owning a luxury does not only potentially influence the social status perception by others but also by oneself. We suggest that this double function that combines intrinsic and extrinsic effects is a key driver for purchasing luxury. Additionally, luxury signal perception depends on preconditions of the receptor as well as the "offensiveness" of the category.

The fundamental frame of luxury signaling can be summarized as follows (see also Figure 8 for visualization):

A luxury good emits a status signal: it carries information about the social status of the person the luxury is connected to. This information is attributed to the owner or consumer. The signal is processed and perceived by oneself (owner or consumer) and by others like the owner's peers. Signal clarity, signal strength, consistency of signals (signal properties) and individual preconditions (receptor properties) influence the signal's perception. Additional important influencing factors are the balance between showing-off and consuming discreetly (luxury expertise) and the category offensiveness (category properties).

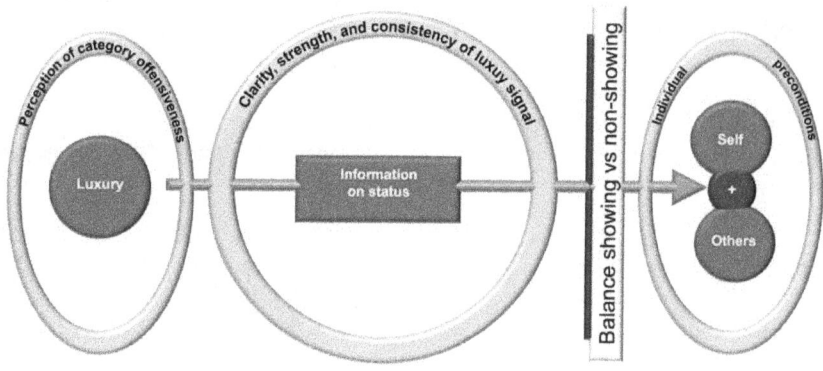

Figure 8: Fundamental Frame of Luxury Signaling

Chapter 4: A Framework of Luxury

Objective:
Combine luxury key concepts into a general framework of luxury

Key aspects:
- Outline of the general framework of luxury
- Description of fundamental structure of "luxury construct"
- Added Luxury Value (ALV) as dependent variable of luxury signal
- Wheel of luxury – anticipated or perceived effects
- Luxury as group marker
- "1%" assumption

ALV and Luxury Signaling

The starting point for a general framework of luxury is the assumption that a bundle of distinct tangible or intangible factors leads to the universal perception that a specific brand or product is "luxury". Those factors will be referred to as "antecedents" of luxury. The rationale is that they occur as preconditions before or "ex ante" the perception of luxury. We provide a comprehensive set of antecedents in this book. Langer & Heil (2013) provides many more examples and rationales beyond those presented here.

Assuming that the preconditions or antecedents indeed lead to the perception of luxury, then a luxury signal with status information would be emitted. If this signal is received and processed, it leads to the perception of added luxury value. ALV summarizes, in a sense, the total perceived value of all social status effects defined by the luxury. Figure 9 provides a visualization of the general framework for luxury.

Why is this framework important from our point of view? We suggest that it is able to describe the fundamental structure of the luxury construct by linking causes and effects. A construct is a variable that cannot be measured directly. This is the case for luxury. To describe and measure it, observable indicators or items are needed. To measure the items and relate them to the luxury construct, the relationship of items and the construct needs to be framed and modeled. As starting point, we identified a clear structural connection between antecedents leading to a luxury signal, which causes the perception of added luxury value. In a nutshell, ALV is the dependent variable of the luxury signal.

We further suggest that the luxury signal is prone to external effects. Those are effects that can enhance or weaken the signal. In our framework those effects are suggested to be moderating variables or moderators. Our rationale is that even under their influence the structure of the relationship within the framework remains unchanged. What changes is the amplitude. Hence, a positive effect remains structurally positive and vice versa. We suggest as important moderators the sender and the situations in which a luxury good is purchased or consumed.

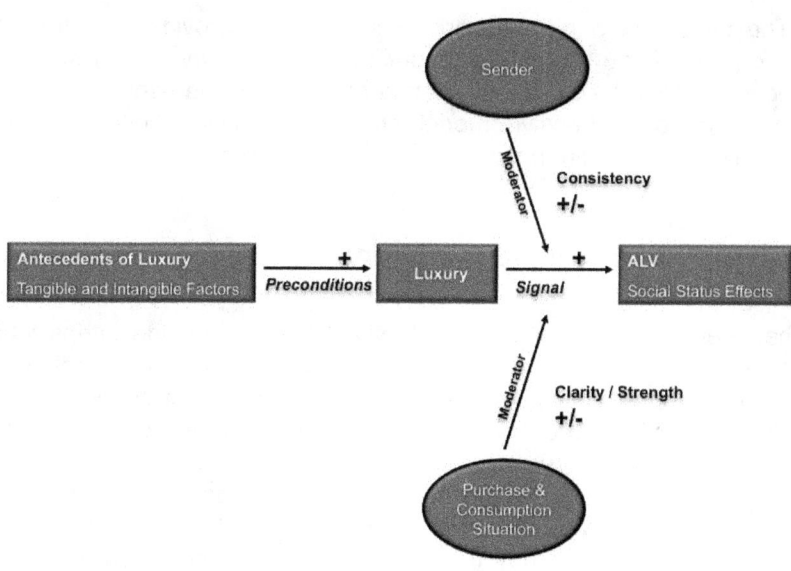

Figure 9: General Framework of Luxury: Luxury Signaling and ALV

A sender is a person who owns or uses the luxury good. The more he or she acts consistently following an individual luxury consumption pattern (see Proposition P4.4), the easier the signal will be perceived with less distortion or moderation. On the other hand, strong inconsistencies in the consumption pattern or other adverse behaviors of the sender, lead to signal moderation towards others.

Purchase and consumption situations are important because they are the points where the luxury is experienced by the owner and eventually by others and where social interactions take place. A Rolex watch that would be sold at a flea market in huge quantities at a low price would obviously send a different, weaker signal compared to the same watch sold in an exclusive environment with exclusive top-notch service at a high price point.

This underlines that the moderating variables are an important part of the framework as they are suggested to be both: able to significantly weaken an otherwise strong luxury signal. Likewise, the moderators may also boost the signal.

The benefit of our framework of luxury is to provide the structural relationship of the input and output factors of luxury. It will serve as conceptual base for further dissecting and framing the aspects of luxury towards a comprehensive model and for identifying how the luxury perception can be influenced, managed and steered.

Intrinsic and Extrinsic Functions

What are the effects of the luxury signal? What are the intrinsic and extrinsic functions of luxury? To move further towards decoding the hidden luxury functions, we look at the statement of a focus group participant, giving his definition of luxury (Businesswire 2004). Like any qualitative study, a focus group is not representative. However, it allows an insight-driven view on luxury. The participant describes luxury as a "state of mind, being able to do what I could not do before. Luxury means I can live my life in a way that I don't have to worry about money. It means to be able to do things in regard to services, time, material things."

There are two insights: First, the insight of being able to do things that could not be done before. Or said in another way: things that cannot be done by others. Thus it could be seen as mind-set change, leading to an improvement in social status. Second, luxury is seen as the ability to choose freely between alternatives.

Let's start with the first insight, the mind-set change towards new experiences. We suggest that luxury goods enable to live and realize dreams. By doing so, the person's personality is influenced and extended in a way to experiment new things.

A person who is not very outgoing and self-confident might change his or her behavior by dressing up in highly fashionable luxury fabrics. Also in this case we expect that the willingness to behave differently would increase and that as a result the person would become more outgoing and confident. Here again, the trigger would have been the luxury goods. We suggest that the mind-set change can go as far as significantly adding self-esteem to a person.

We suggest that luxuries, due to a certain difficulty in consuming, attribute the consumer with an "expert" status of being a "connoisseur". Rationale is that certain luxuries may require a certain expertise in selection, utilization and appreciation.

Let us return to the insight study and its second implication: luxury as a signal of being able to choose freely among alternatives. Directionally, this status could be described as "freedom of choice" status, hence a situation of financial liquidity or economic power. A luxury therefore signals that the owner can afford it economically and probably would still be able to afford other things. As this signal is attributed to its owner, it is independent of the true status. We suggest that this is of strong importance as "...money enlarges the sense of self because it enlarges imaginable possibilities of all we might have and do" (Belk 1988, p.150).

This adds a very important facet to luxury: it communicates social dominance. If someone is financially able to do what he or she wants – hence, ability to execute a choice – and if a luxury good signals this ability, then as a consequence, a luxury product plays an important role in defining the social position. In line with this finding, Pincus (2004, p.380) links "materialism, social comparison processes, lifestyle/value" to the personality traits of luxury items.

Looking at the extreme, one might say that luxury is able to make ugly people look better. For normal people it might simply become a head-turner, due to signaling more attractiveness. An indication is the wide appearance of luxury handbags, luxury luggage or other "decorative" luxury items.

If the owner believes that he or she is more attractive, it should further enhance the self-confidence and improve social chances. In this sense, luxury enhances self-perception.

A facet of enhanced self-perception is suggested to be the strengthening of perceived individuality. We further suggest that, as a result of increased self-esteem, self-perception, self-confidence, individuality and social dominance, a luxury product provides the ultimate social protection and social shelter. In a sense, this can be interpreted by the equation that no other product is able to offer better social protection because no other product is better.

What does it mean? If a person owns or utilizes a luxury, the product signals that he or she will be protected from negative thoughts or comments of peers, due to the fact that he or she utilizes simply the ultimate product. Thus, the social shelter is a protective function that increases the potential range of acting in the surrounding social setting.

A derivate of being the ultimate protector is the attribution of decision-quality, which we also see correlated with connoisseurship. We suggest that luxury signals a high degree of decision expertise when it comes to purchases. In short: In case of uncertainty, the best becomes a rather safe choice.

As we see luxury goods as part of the hedonic product set, they provide by nature hedonic attributes like fun and enjoyment. Concerning luxuries we suggest that those attributes may even reach as far as to provide unique mental and physical experiences.

We, therefore, propose that luxury products may serve as the ultimate treat or instant gratification. That can be seen also as a typical reward for hard work, graduation, and special achievements or simply to underline one's individuality.

The root idea of perceived or anticipated effects of the luxury signal has led to a set of important luxury aspects. The set is visualized in Figure 10. We will refer to it as "Wheel of Luxury". As rationale we suggest that the luxury aspects may be somewhat correlated and interdependent; one aspect might interrelate with others or even strengthen them. However, they are all effects of a common cause: the signal emitted by the luxury.

We further suggest that the intrinsic and extrinsic functions are rather exclusive to luxuries, at least in combined appearance. They are important contributors to the total perceived added luxury value. Thus, they should be part of a comprehensive luxury definition.

Religions often condemn excesses in owning or consuming goods; the same applies to some political ideas like communism. People who actively and consciously follow those norms and rules might process luxury signals in a different way from others.

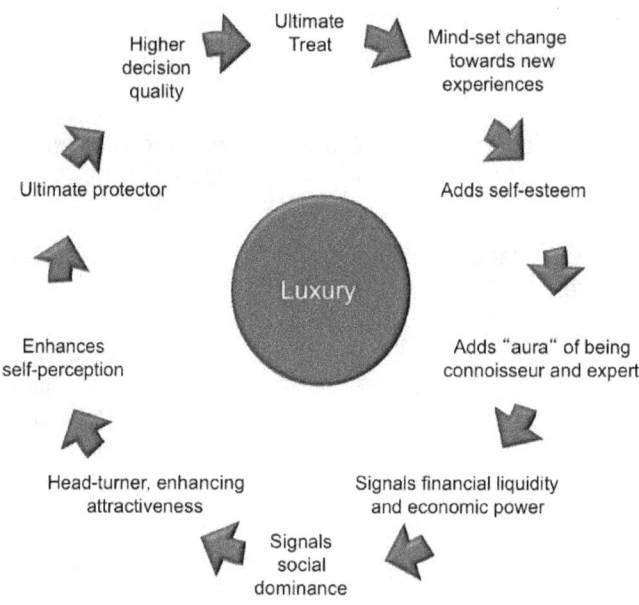

Figure 10: "Wheel of Luxury" – Luxury's Hidden Aspects Decoded

51

Group Marker: Luxury as Identification Code of Groups

So far we concluded that luxury has the ability to define, shape and improve the individual position in the social context. This leads to the suggestion that luxury goods have also an important function as identifiers within social groups. In a sense, they could be seen as "ID codes". This means that those "contextually used" luxury products have the function of a "marker" for that social group.

Looking from a different angle, luxury can also be the entrance ticket to certain groups because distinct group contexts might require the use of distinct luxury goods. In a sense, we suggest that a luxury product can be the commonly "minimum expected product" in a certain social context.

Luxury Categories and Category Position

It is obvious that different wealth situations will lead to different financially accessible categories with hypothetical extremes of toilet paper on one end and a private jet on the other end.

As individual starting points, individual preference sets as well as social contexts will differ from person to person, we indicate that luxury products could be found theoretically in most – if not all – product categories. Dubois et al. (2005, p.115) also suggest this, referring luxury "to a specific tier of offer in almost any product or service category". It is an important implication for managers, as luxury products within each category need to be managed properly to signal the above-described attributes.

The indication that all categories could have luxury products contrasts with some classic views on luxury, where luxury product categories are seen as few selected ones, such as fashion with its luxury sub-segment haute couture, perfumery, jewelry, watches, leather goods, shoes, cars, wine, champagne, spirits, tableware, crystal and porcelain (see Dubois and Duquesne 1993). However, we argue that in most of those "classical luxury" categories, luxury goods as well as non-luxury goods exist. Other categories that might not be associated with luxury at first sight, such as dishwashing, mobile phones or bottled water, could still have a luxury sub-segment. Therefore we suggest that luxury is in general category-independent. We had a closer inspection on this conclusion in our category assessment of luxury in Chapter 2.

As luxuries may be found in all product categories, it is important to define a general rule – applicable for different categories – at which point a "normal" product ends and "luxury" begins. To make this operational we need to make some assumptions.

Given a typical category with several competing brands and products, we assume normal distribution of prices of the several offers. Only the absolute top end products along the price range in each category are suggested to be able to signal significant ALV.

Therefore we propose that typically only goods belonging to the top 1% of all goods of a category along the price dimension have the potential to be luxury goods. This is shown in Figure 11.

The proposition is consistent with the reality in product categories where a luxury segment clearly exists, for example luxury watches or luxury phones. In those segments, the few top brands on the price dimension, such as Rolex or Patek Philippe, account for 1%-2% of the category sales, however they may account for up to 30% of the industry value (The New Zealand Herald, Oct 20, 2006). In the luxury segment for mobile phones, Vertu sells phones with prices up to €300,000, while the sales quantities are very low, for some models below ten on a global level.

The proposition that luxury – in a narrow understanding of the term – is typically limited to the absolute top tier of a category in terms of price, often far away from other brands and offers of that category, clearly indicates how significant and large the perceived added luxury value can become in consumer's perceptions and evaluations.

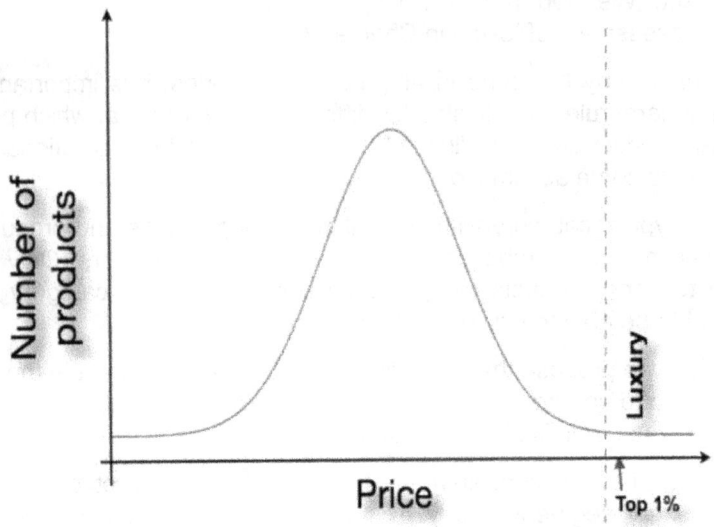

Required parameters are missing or incorrect.

Figure 11: 1% Assumption for Luxury Goods

We suggest that including more goods to the luxury "basket", e.g. the top 5% or the 10% of all goods of a category, would decrease the precision of an operational luxury definition significantly. It is likely that some of those goods would not unanimously belong to luxuries anymore.

Those goods would be rather premium or even normal hedonic goods, typically not able to provide significant added luxury value. The almost ubiquitous use of the term luxury, even for normal goods, suggests that it is often utilized outside its narrow context and done so with little precision.

> **Assuming normal distribution of prices within a category, we propose that generally the top 1% of all goods along the price dimension have the potential to be luxury goods.**

In a sense, there are limitations to the 1% rule, especially for goods that have no price transparency. An original painting by a famous artist, let's say Picasso, that is not traded and that therefore has no price, is difficult to classify. A large house at the seaside of a fancy city might trigger an immediate luxury perception, while the actual price could be cheap.

However, as exceptions will be rather limited for most product categories, we clearly suggest the narrow definition approach due to its sharpness.

Chapter 5: What is Luxury, Really?

Objective:
Precisely defining luxury

Key aspects:
- Core definition of luxury
- Extended luxury definition
- Visualization of the luxury definition
- Inverse Pyramid Model of luxury consumption
- Assessment of the luxury definition

Condensing our luxury propositions, we frame an operational definition of luxury. It has the objective to be sharp and precise. In our core definition we focus on key aspects, in an extended definition we reflect all major aspects of the luxury construct.

Core Definition

Luxury is something rare and hedonic, difficult to acquire or use, that provides a perceived unique experience in combination with a perceived enhancement or reinforcement of the social position. It is an emotional social marker and differentiator.

Luxuries may be durable or non-durable products and services. Although time is often referred to as luxury, we propose that time is not a luxury because time does not enhance or reinforce the social position per se. However, time may be spent on an experience that is perceived as luxury.

Extended Definition

A luxury is something rare that is able to signal status information. The signal can be received and processed by the owner and by others depending on signal clarity, strength and consistency. The signal has the effect to trigger the perception of an enhancement or reinforcement of the social status. It results in a perceived consumer value, the added luxury value ALV, which can become the major value component of a luxury product's total value for a consumer. ALV is composed of enhanced self-esteem, self-perception and attractiveness, attribution of financial liquidity, social power and expertise, protection in public and the perception of new, unique and ultimate experiences by a hedonic good that functions as ultimate treat. Additionally, a luxury is a social marker, classifying people as members of distinct social groups. As a reflection of added luxury value, luxuries tend to be overly expensive, they are difficult to purchase or use. Typically they belong to the top 1% cluster of the most expensive goods or services in a category. Luxuries tend to be compatible with social norms and values, a precondition for status reassurance.

In a nutshell, luxury is something unique and thus desirable which is difficult to get and may be difficult to handle, manage or use. Therefore it triggers a world of dreams. As it sends a signal that is processed by the owner and by others, it is able to evoke a status reassurance in the eye of both: from the perspective of the owner as well as from the perspective of others. This can be the surrounding social group including the owner's peers. The definition is visualized in Figure 12.

The uncertainty principle of luxury suggests that the perception of a good being a luxury remains individual, depending on the individual purchasing power and the accumulated ownership, consumption experiences and current social status.

The function as social marker and differentiator is expected to partly offset the individual views, as culturally common codes and perceptions on luxury have to exist, otherwise the social signal would not be working. Lindner (2008) cites Harvard professor John Gourville noting, "...that what passes as sophisticated in one area might be considered average in another. For instance, he says that a Mercedes in his middle-class suburb of Boston might turn heads, but the same car in Beverly Hills would not." Thus, the social reference group is decisive for the choice of luxury items.

Luxury's ability to signal an enhanced status of its owner towards himself and others could also be a trigger to evoke negative associations among others, such as envy or even hatred. In this context, the fear of being seen as show-off could be a serious hurdle for a luxury purchase. It may evoke the feeling of guilt, which might discourage one from purchasing a luxury item or service.

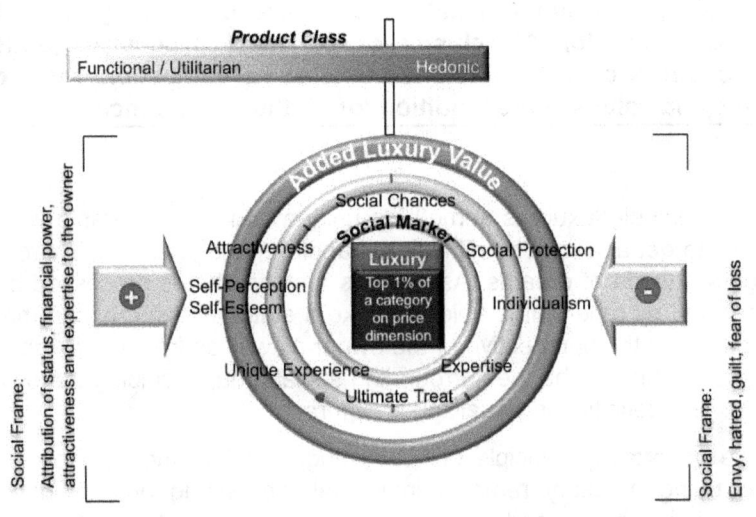

Figure 12: Luxury Definition

We suggest that actual or potential negative effects build a limiting social frame to luxury (see Figure 12). From our point of view it is important to steer this limiting frame properly in managing luxury in a sustainable and profitable way.

Satisfaction of Needs: The Inverse Pyramid Model

As we concluded that luxury is a deep personal need relevant to practically every person, individual purchasing power and product expertise influence how many and which luxuries may be purchased or consumed. With this rationale and following Belk's (1985) findings on shifts on materialism over lifespan, we suggest a luxury consumption hierarchy model, which may be described with consumption and experience related clusters. We refer to this hierarchy as the inverse pyramid model of luxury (see Figure 13).

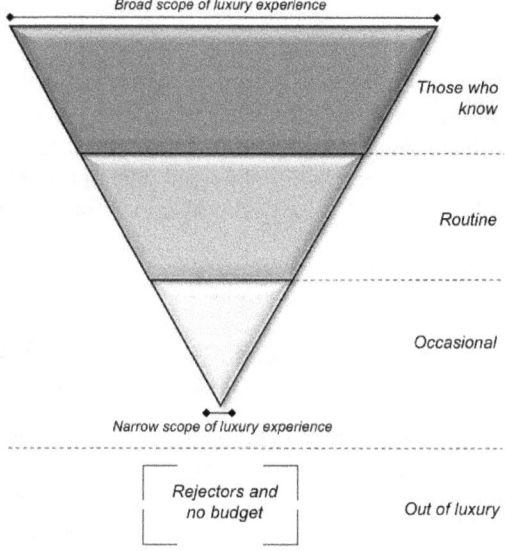

Figure 13: Inverse Pyramid Model of Luxury

Some consumers stay out of luxury. The group consists of people who categorically reject luxuries and who would not buy them for their individual specific reasons. A monk would be a good example. We suggest that even a billionaire almost without spending limitations for most categories would not buy luxuries if he or she consciously rejected them.

Also those people without a budget to afford luxury goods would fall into this cluster. If a person has no or very limited financial power and limited product expertise, similar to the lowest level in Maslow's need hierarchy, luxury consumption will be limited to pure desire: the person desires luxuries and would buy them, however he or she cannot afford them.

When the scope of luxury consumption broadens with increasing financial opportunities, we expect very selective consumption of some luxury goods. Those goods could also include some premium products outside of the narrow definition of luxury, but still perceived as luxuries from an individual standpoint. We suggest referring to this consumption pattern as "occasional" luxury consumption.

Increase of financial power and product expertise is suggested to lead to purchasing more luxury goods. People acquire a certain "routine" in luxury consumption and experience: luxuries are purchased and consumed regularly and become an integral part of the individual lifestyle. By this, and with increased luxury signal consistency, luxuries fulfill the social marker function.

At a certain point luxury consumption gets beyond "routine", beyond "usual" luxury consumption. We cluster this group of consumers as "those who know": people extremely experienced with luxury in such a way that they may even not perceive certain high-end products as luxury anymore.

In financial terms this could be high-net-worth-individuals or even ultra-high-net-worth-individuals who may own several planes, a yacht, and houses, have a collection of luxury cars and watches. "Having it all", they often turn away from known brands and become experts in specific areas of interest, where they try to discover the best brands in the world and order their products fitting to their most individual needs. To most people those companies and brands would be practically unknown, as they tend to produce goods "made to measure" to a very limited clientele.

In the inverse pyramid model, there is not necessarily always an upgrading. It is also possible that people "start" in one of the higher clusters, e.g. by being born into a rich family. Likewise, it is possible that people move "down", e.g. if they lose their fortune and simply cannot afford anymore to be in luxury routine.

With each upgrade from one cluster to another, we suggest the luxury consumption to have increasingly discreet and unique characteristics, at least in part, to help overcoming the dilemma between the need to show in order to signal and the danger to show-off. Still, even with part of the consumption being discreet, the luxury consumption of a person with a high routine in luxury consumption will likely be identifiable by others.

We suggest that the consumption behavior summarized in the inverse pyramid model is a direct result of our proposition on signal consistency. The more consistent the signal becomes, the better the status information of a luxury good can be perceived and processed. As signal perception and processing are also important to the owner, the individual added luxury value should increase due to positive moderation (see framework in Figure 9). Therefore, also due to the increasing value perception, we suggest that people will tend to increase the percentage of luxuries within their total consumption basket in correlation with increased wealth and spending possibilities.

Assessment of the Definition

While being consistent with the research status quo, e.g. high price, hedonism, pleasure, ease, or personality extension, we introduced several new luxury aspects and propositions, broadening the framework of luxury (see Table 4). We also distilled and revealed a set of "hidden" aspects of luxury.

First, our definition provides a "reason why" or "reason to be" for a luxury good. It is a result of a key concept that we introduced: the concept of luxury signaling as one fundamental base for luxury. In short we propose that luxuries are able to evoke changes in status perception, both intrinsically and extrinsically.

It leads to a fundamentally new view: luxuries are important to people due to two expected outcomes: One, the perception of the own status enhancement perceived by the person himself or herself. Two, the perception of the own status upgrading expected to be perceived by others. The traditional view on luxury rather as "conspicuous" consumption focuses mainly on the latter.

The luxury signal concept is further able to explain the dilemma between the necessity to show in order to have a perceivable signal and the danger to show-off, leading to discreet luxury alongside increased luxury consumption. We further explain the purchase and consumption motivation through the effect of the signal, e.g. signaling an elevated social status, higher self-perception or increased chances. All those fundamental intrinsic and extrinsic aspects of luxury were identified as "wheel of luxury" (see Figure 10).

Table 4: Assessment of the Luxury Definition

Aspects of our Luxury Definition	Factors and Aspects from previous Definitions	Broadened Framework
Hedonic good	» Pleasure and indulgence. » Ease and comfort. » Experience providing. » Luxuries retain or improve category functionalities.	» Continuum: Functional aspects are provided; however, hedonic items over- proportionally perceived.
Luxury Signaling	» Conspicuous consumption. » Status symbols.	» Luxuries send status information signal. » Signal processing depends on signal clarity, strength and consistency. » Compatibility with social norms. » Signal can be processed by oneself and others. » Too much "showing-off" can decrease luxury perception. » Tendency towards discreet luxury. » Correlation between signal and perceived ALV.

Aspects of our Luxury Definition	Factors and Aspects from previous Definitions	Broadened Framework
Added luxury value (ALV):	» Pleasure. » Experience providing » Distinct product qualities: design, aesthetics, style, materials, scarcity, and history. » Means of differentiation. » Extend personality.	» Mind-set change towards new experiences. » Add self-esteem. » Expert "aura". » Signal of financial liquidity. » Signal of social dominance » Head turner. » Enhanced self-perception and attractiveness. » Ultimate protector and social shelter. » Increased decision quality. » In sum, reason why for luxury purchase.
Social Marker	» Income. » Culture. » Social class. » Social values. » Segmentation. » Snob and bandwagon effects. » Something difficult to use. » "Elite group"	» Attributing people as members of social groups. » Luxuries can be minimum expected products of a social group. » Risk of evoking negative associations (e.g. envy, hate). » Risk of lowering social status by losing item. » Additional reason why for luxury.
Sub-segment of hypothetically every product category	» Sub set of various product categories.	» Theoretically, all segments can have a luxury tier.
Satisfaction of need	» Not absolutely necessary. » Necessity-luxury continuum.	» Necessary for many due to exclusive ability to signal status.
Uncertainty principle of luxury	» Social values. » Luxury depends on individual views and experiences.	» Individuality remains, however social marker function suggests common codes and perceptions.
Top 1% of products of its category along price dimension	» Expensive. » Highest in terms of quality and price. » Income elasticity.	» Narrow, precise definition within a category.

Luxuries function by improving the social status quo while providing exceptional experiences. They have the ability to socially uplift the owner in parallel to the ability to reinforce his or her social group membership, being a group marker. We suggest these abilities to be regarded as fundamental ownership and consumption motivations.

Secondly and closely related to the first finding, luxuries satisfy needs and are therefore relevant for most people. In the most basic terms, all members of a society strive for biological reproduction. Luxuries function consciously or unconsciously as a social facilitator, as they signal the elevated social position and power.

The view that luxuries satisfy basic needs contrasts with some classic definitions of luxuries being either non-essential goods or being relevant to few people only. Instead, we described the inverse pyramid model of luxury consumption from occasional towards an individual luxury lifestyle ("those who know"). This is a logic result from our proposition of signal consistency. The finding also broadens the possibilities to market luxuries and suggests the importance of professionally managing luxuries, based on deep consumer understanding, segmentation or targeted communication.

The ability to satisfy a need also explains the "democratization" of luxury, which is increasingly mentioned in papers and articles: it does not seem to be a new phenomenon per se, but a result of more available wealth and probably also of extended luxury offers in more accessible categories.

Different purchasing power and different social codes, experiences and habits will lead to different relevant luxury product categories. The frequent purchase of luxury items might well lead to a "luxury living" which may be seen as rather excessive by some (see Kivetz and Simonson 2002a). Nonetheless, we argue that the core motivation for purchasing a luxury good lies in its social function in terms of uplifting and marking, thus satisfying needs.

Third, we introduced the key concept of added luxury value ALV as exclusive value of luxuries, strongly correlated with the status signaling ability. We postulate that among non-luxuries even premium products send a significantly weaker, less evident and less efficient status signal. As a result, ALV is able to explain the significant price premiums for luxuries. We suggest that losing a luxury item has a strong negative influence on the owner and his or her state of mind, as ALV "evaporates". Therefore luxury seems to require higher quality and durability. Also a stable social and economic environment will facilitate luxury purchase and consumption.

Fourth, we argue with Dubois et al. (2005) that luxury can be found in all categories, at least hypothetically. As this would lead to an infinite number of products an operational criteria is needed to enhance the precision of a definition of luxury. As criteria, we suggest that only very few products of each category, the top 1% of a category measured on the price dimension, have the potential to be luxury products in a narrow interpretation of the term. We further broaden the framework, suggesting that in certain categories luxuries might be perceived as more offensive compared to the "basic" products. A higher perceived offensiveness may trigger counter-reactions by other people. The phenomenon is evident looking at the worldwide discussion about fuel economy and CO_2 emissions of heavy luxury SUVs.

The high price tag of a luxury product is an important indicator to identify a luxury. It may also often be one of the key reasons for purchasing as a high price helps to separate apart from others. However, our propositions and definition suggest clearly that price is not the exclusive indicator: the high price of luxuries is rather a result of the perceived added luxury value. Apart from the price that sets luxuries apart, they are typically somewhat more difficult to obtain or they may require usage premiums.

To manage luxury profitably, it will be essential to analyze all its key facets in detail. We will focus on this in the following section. Then, we will specifically look at pricing as the monetary measure of the added luxury value.

Chapter 6: What Drives Luxury?

Objective:
Provide a comprehensive overview on drivers of luxury perception

Key aspects:
- Set of facets commonly understood as being part of luxury
- Drivers have high importance for luxury perception

Now we look at those facets that are "driving" the luxury perception: a set of facets that are commonly understood as being "part" of luxury and its experience. If they are present, at least in part, then the likelihood of connecting a product with luxury increases. Those facets can either be antecedents of luxury or they can be connected to expected or perceived effects of luxury. Therefore we suggest their high importance for the perception of luxury, and thus call them "luxury drivers". An overview on all dimensions and groups of luxury drivers is shown in Table 5.

In the following chapters we will give an overview of the drivers of each of the six dimensions and discuss their importance of driving the perceived value of a luxury good. While we present all drivers in this book, we suggest Langer & Heil (2013) to those who want to go deeper and get more examples on how luxury brands manage the drivers successfully.

Table 5: Overview of Dimensions and Groups of Luxury Drivers

Dimension	Groups of Luxury Drivers
Product and experience related	1. Luxury drivers related to quality and aesthetics.
	2. Luxury drivers related to the purchase situation of a luxury.
	3. Luxury drivers related to the consumption situation of a luxury.
Socially related	4. Luxury drivers related to the cultural and social frame.
Segment related	5. Luxury drivers related to consumer segments.
Awareness and equity related	6. Luxury drivers related to product and brand awareness.

Chapter 7: Quality and Aesthetics

Objective:
Dissection of luxury drivers related to quality and aesthetics of products and services

Key aspects:
- Uniqueness and individualization drive luxury perception
- Rare materials and special refinement as luxury drivers
- Luxuries as "Piece of Art"
- Focus on every detail of aesthetics drives value perception
- Creation of unique experiences and pleasure drives luxury
- Features and top-in-class performance on few items help to educate
- Top-in-class quality perception is of utmost importance

Luxury is most often connected to an extraordinary product quality. It is obvious that a wine will only become a precious and luxurious vintage wine if it provides an extraordinary taste and if not too many bottles exist. The same is true for a top-end leather bag, which requires a perfect material finish and few available items.

We suggested that high quality and durability are also important since losing a valuable luxury or not being able to use it anymore would have a strong impact on both, the owner's self-perception and the perception by others. Dubois et al. (2001, p.8) even propose that quality and luxury are practically synonymous for some people. One respondent of their study highlights: "For me luxury means quality".

Table 6 summarizes different drivers of luxury that we distilled related to the extraordinary quality and aesthetics of luxury goods. They include drivers, such as individualization, detail focus, specialized items, strict rules for aesthetics, top-in-class performance, and experience.

Table 6: Luxury Drivers – Quality and Aesthetics

Driver	Luxury Drivers Related to Quality and Aesthetics
D1.1	Uniqueness of a good due to strong individualization and special crafting techniques.
D1.2	Utilization of rare and expensive materials with high requirements in manufacturing expertise.
D1.3	Focus on every detail, creating a feeling of extreme refinement.
D1.4	Utilization of "craftsmanship signals", e.g. highly specialized items that very few experts manage to build and service.
D1.5	Prominent utilization of logos as "craftsmanship signals".
D1.6	Special aesthetics of refinement, excitement, class, style and sophistication add a unique value.
D1.7	Highly refined and carefully designed packaging.
D1.8	Strict rules and codes for every detail of the aesthetics.
D1.9	Specially crafted features beyond usual aesthetics and design.
D1.10	Consistency of the context of luxury purchasing and usage: refined aesthetics in presenting the product and refined aesthetics connected to the people buying and utilizing the product.
D1.11	Crafting a good to potentially become a piece of art.
D1.12	Top-in-class performance in its specific expertise area.
D1.13	Top-in-class experience.
D1.14	Celebrities, royals and known "experts" utilize the product.
D1.15	Being perceived as one of a kind.
D1.16	Limited availability through clear connection to an event, a purchase history, a person.
D1.17	Positioning a product in a way to become "history" by being ultimately unique and famous.
D1.18	Perceived consistency in superior quality.
D1.19	Heritage and image: luxuries have a story or even a legend.

Uniqueness and Individualization

Examples for extraordinary craftsmanship driving the perception of luxury are products that are individually produced, made-to-measure, or handcrafted to unique specifications. Those efforts result in highly individualized products, which may exist only once. Belk's research in possessions (1988, p.144) explains the appeal of individualized products with the "psychic energy" that is invested by the owner in taking part in the creation process. "This energy and its products are regarded as part of self because they have grown or emerged from the self."

Possessing something that exists only once in the world – e.g. a painting – or experiencing a service that has the potential of being a once-in-a-lifetime experience have the ability to make the owner more individual, more distinctive. It separates him or her from others among the social reference group. It is also a reflection of the owner's attitude of wanting to add a little touch of him or herself. It states clearly "I am unique".

Rare Materials and Items in Combination with Special Refinement

Not surprisingly, rare, individual and expensive materials like gold, diamonds and other precious stones, leathers or wood are often used for luxury products. They require special manufacturing expertise including handcrafting.

The touch of exclusivity can be clearly enhanced by rare materials or unique production expertise. A great example is Audemars Piguet, a Swiss luxury watch maker, that was able to repeatedly reinforce its unique positioning of exquisite refinement by inventing some of the world's thinnest complicated movements. As a result, they are able to offer complicated watches that combine elegance and craftsmanship. Furthermore, with their Royal Oak watch-face, Audemars Piguet owns one of the most unique, recognizable and beautiful designs of all time.

We suggest that both, rather hedonic materials and special crafting methods have a strong driving force in building the luxury perception. This is confirmed in the study of Dubois et al. (2001, p.8–9), where ingredients or components as well as delicacy and expertise involved in manufacturing came out as major indicators for quality, "...with every detail being important. When total perfection is achieved, a feeling of extreme refinement emerges". They suggest that at the extreme end, there is the perception that a luxury product could be used forever, giving a feeling of eternity.

Often certain "craftsmanship signals" are used. We suggest that their main function is to visualize the extraordinary craftsmanship skills used to produce the luxury watch. Examples are tourbillions for exclusive watches: they have a very distinct shape, easy to be recognized. Thus, tourbillions are typically placed prominently on the front side. For the owner and for others the feature strongly highlights: "This watch was crafted by the best watchmakers".

In the case of cars, such "craftsmanship signals" could be ceramic brakes, which Porsche is offering as one of a handful of companies. Yes, they provide a better performance than a classic brake. However, it is questionable if the pure performance increase is the main motivation to pay a premium that is similar to the value of a small car. Instead, the special brake is clearly visible from the outside at least for car experts and easily detectable due to special color code and shape. Also here an important purchase motivation might be to signal towards others: "I drive a car with a feature that very few other people have and that few companies are able to build".

In some categories it is difficult to differentiate through materials and items alone. This is the case for handbags. Of course it is possible to utilize very rare leathers or to incorporate diamonds, but for a highly fashionable item like a handbag also common materials – like denim – are used in the luxury segment. The same goes for dresses, where often the omission of fabrics may lead to a more luxurious product. Where materials are not necessarily an easy differentiator between luxuries and normal goods, other facets have to come in place.

For handbags and fashion items, craftsmanship and expertise in selecting and combining materials is often signaled simply by prominently placing the brand logo. Louis Vuitton, Hermès or Chanel are typical examples.

Here, instead of a watch's tourbillion, the logo is utilized from our point of view rather in a function as a "craftsmanship" or "expertise" signal and not only in marking the sender. Thus, independent if a bag is made of leather or denim, people have the reassurance that the product is luxury because of Louis Vuitton's, Hermès' or Chanel's expertise in crafting bags.

In sum, rare and expensive materials, highly specialized items or even simply a prominent brand logo influence the luxury perception. We assume that the sharper and better a company designs those attributes, the clearer and stronger luxury signals will be perceived. While it is hypothetically possible to build a luxury product with atypical materials or items – take a luxury watch made of plastic and featuring a rubber wristband – it is extremely unlikely.

Luxury Aesthetics Creating a Unique Value

Luxury aesthetics are important for the spontaneous and repeated quality perception of a luxury good. They include colors, packaging, logo, typography and all other visual, audible, olfactory, tactile or even taste experiences (see Lageat et al. 2003 for the engineering of hedonic attributes).

The aesthetics strongly influence the total product experience and evaluation. It is obvious that aesthetics that are perceived as "ordinary, boring, outdated, unsophisticated and cheap" will hardly signal "luxury". Instead, if the product design stands for "refinement, excitement, class, style and sophistication", the luxury signal should become clearer.

One important part of the aesthetics is the packaging, which is the reason why many luxury goods are packaged in an extraordinary way. Think of the cases for high-end watches, often luxury products themselves.

The luxury packaging aspect is not limited to packaging or boxes. Also the core products are usually very carefully designed to the very last detail. Dom Perignon comes in a very distinct bottle with a unique label, that signals tradition, quality and class, or: "This champagne is one of its kind". Each Hermès scarf has a very carefully created design, which is so typical that it can be distinguished as "by Hermès" even without seeing the logo.

We suggest that crafting the aesthetics to the smallest detail results in a very unique experience, providing a unique value to consumers. In short, luxuries can be seen as a source of unique sensual experiences and pleasure.

We argued before that any product category could hypothetically have luxury offerings. In this context it can be key to utilize specially crafted features beyond the usual aesthetics. Let's think of a hypothetical luxury toilet paper, sold for $2,000 a roll. No one would pay the luxury premium if there were no distinction to a $0.30 roll. Neither would anyone perceive ALV. A possible "luxury" distinction could be utilizing paper designed by artists, with an individual design on each paper section. Instead of using board, each roll could be wrapped around a gold-plated tube, each with an individual pattern, designed to be collected once the role is finished. Each role could be numbered, the availability strictly limited. With such a setup, a price of $2,000 per item could be hypothetically achieved even in the toilet paper category.

Luxuries as "Pieces of Art"

Dubois et al. (2001, p.12–13) extract that luxury consumers may go that far to expect:

- Refined aesthetics from the entire context in which luxury products are presented.
- Equally refined aesthetics from the people who consume the luxury goods.

This supports our proposition on consistency of the luxury signal: The more consistent the context – from point of sale up to the styling and attitude of people buying or using a luxury item -, the more authentic the sensual experience may become.

Luxury as a sensual and very unique experience can go quite far: "At the extreme, luxury products become pieces of art which have to be recognized as such" (Dubois et al. 2001, p.12). Willis (2007, online) cites the manager of the Royal de Versailles Jewellers, with a similar opinion on the Panerai tourbillion that takes more than 2 years to build: "They are pieces of art, or the equivalent of a Rolls-Royce."

It seems that a luxury product can really be compared with a piece of art. Indicators are prices that are paid for selected luxury items at auctions. The Henry Graves Super Grande Complication pocket watch from Patek Philippe was sold for $11 million (Business Insider 2012, online), the highest price ever paid for a watch in any auction to that point in time, thus ranging similar to drawings of Rembrandt. Other vintage watches from Patek Philippe or Breguet may achieve prices up to $4 million. Collectors often expose those items at their homes similar to a painting. They are typically insured and even protected by alarm systems. Such a vintage watch would probably never ever been worn in order to keep its value. Likewise, in 2007, the world's oldest surviving Rolls-Royce, a 1904 10hp two-seater, was auctioned for £3.5 million (Times, Dec 3, 2007). It shows which exceptional perceived value unique brands like Rolls-Royce have been able to create.

Becoming part of collections is also the aim of contemporary limited edition watches of luxury watch brands, often priced far above €100,000 and typically produced in series below 20. Also those watches would rarely been worn. Instead they would normally be kept as investment or simply as a means of pleasure and admiration.

Also vintage cars, like the 1950s Mercedes 300 SL, have become pieces in museums and are featured in glossy art-books.

The suggestion that luxuries and art go hand in hand becomes also obvious in the architecture of some luxury spaces that are now often designed by leading architects. On the product side, Louis Vuitton has been repeatedly teaming up with artists like Takashi Murakami or Richard Prince to create new handbag designs that feature art or at least the artist's very individual style. Those collaborations also add a level of surprise to the brand experience and allow further differentiation to an already highly differentiated product.

The aspect of connecting a product with art clearly helps to differentiate a luxury good from other products, adds a "story" and emotion and also might help to prevent fakes, due to its refined crafting and aesthetics.

Product Performance versus Experience

In contrast to the expertise in materials and production, some of the functional product performance items of a luxury product are not necessarily best in class, nor is this necessarily expected. A mechanical luxury watch is not necessarily overly precise in telling the time. In fact, any $20 quartz watch will beat the precision performance of a $300,000 tourbillion watch. Hence, luxury product quality is not necessarily about top-in-class performance of all items or having the very latest features.

However, we suggest that luxuries provide always top-in-class performance in very specific and consumer-relevant expertise areas. The luxury watch might not tell the time more precisely than the quartz watch, however in terms of craftsmanship and aesthetics it will clearly outperform any normal watch.

Luxury is therefore not about top-in-class-performance in many items, but we suggest that it needs to be perceived as top-in-class for at least one key-item in its field of expertise.

Luxury is rather about heritage and expertise in production, utilization of known precious and rare materials, and the overall experience provided to the buyers and consumers. We therefore also expect higher brand loyalty for luxury than for normal products, where functional product features have a higher importance.

We argued before that the total product experience would have a significant influence on the additional luxury value. Therefore steering experiences is important for luxury managers. However, Lageat et al. (2003, p.99) point out that "because of their subjective and experiential nature, the assessment of the sources of hedonic attribute perceptions remains problematic." Reason is that people may not have the required knowledge to appreciate hedonic attributes. An inexperienced wine drinker might simply not distinguish the taste of a luxury wine from a normal one.

The implication for managing luxury is that the luxury experience, and with it the added luxury value, can be influenced by educating the consumers about the special functional and hedonic features of the product. If an unusual luxury material is utilized – think of the example of the hypothetical luxury car with a plastic dashboard – a profound explanation (e.g. higher car performance through less weight) will be required to help setting the context.

If a product requires expertise in manufacturing or consuming, at least in a significantly refined way compared to a basic product of its category, it is likely to signal that the owner has a certain expertise. True or not in terms of knowledge and expertise, the purchase is likely to attribute this expertise to him or her. This should result in an improved perception of social status as suggested before.

A limitation is, however, that the attribution of expertise will only work, if general knowledge about the product, materials or features exists within the social reference group. The cut of a tailored suit might simply not be recognizable by others and the product might not be identified as luxury.

Product quality has also an important function to rationally explain or even excuse a top-of-category investment, spending a significant luxury premium for an item.

This gives the consumer arguments and a rationale to explain his or her purchase, at least with the prospect of a clever investment due to the scarce offer and the famous other owners. Instead of being a simple product, the product becomes part of "history", thus ultimately unique and famous, justifying almost any premium.

Quality Perception

If a luxury brand consistently delivers perceived superior quality and therefore a purchase rationale, it can provide the social shelter of attributing decision quality and expertise related to the purchase, as we suggested before. If a Patek Philippe watch is perceived as the ultimate in watchmaking, providing a stable value and is given from one generation to the other, then who could question the decision quality of the purchase?

We argued that providing joy and excitement is an important function of luxury goods as they may be purchased as ultimate treat. Also in this case, superior product quality is decisive in providing that positive emotion. A luxury car, of which the air condition button gets loose after driving 1,000 miles, will most probably not be able to consistently deliver fun.

To steer the added luxury value, we believe that the purchase reassurance through consistent extraordinary quality and materials, top craftsmanship combined with individual servicing is of utmost importance. If a luxury good is giving no reasons to justify the purchase at the luxury price point, we even expect an adverse effect of decreasing the perceived social status. Rationale is that buying an ultra-expensive product that does not endorse quality or taste might suggest that the owner is simply someone wasting money.

A facet of extraordinary luxury product quality is typically its heritage and image. Dubois et al. (2001) suggest luxuries need to have a story, ideally a legend. This explains why almost all luxury brands stress their heritage as something special and related to the experience.

Summary: Luxury Driver – Quality, Heritage and Aesthetics

Summarizing the findings on product quality, heritage and aesthetics we conclude as follows:

I.   Typically a luxury good has significantly higher manufacturing and individualization requirements in terms of quality, product aesthetics and utilized materials than a normal product. It is typically top-of-class in terms of a unique performance point and provides unique experiences. Higher individualization in the luxury segment should lead to higher consumer loyalty and should positively drive ALV.

II.   Luxury items typically signal consumer expertise. This is driven by refined items, individuality and selected materials. Also the requirement of specific category knowledge, e.g. on how to drive a luxury sports car, signals expertise. The stronger the "expertise signal", the stronger ALV is expected to become.

III. Certain materials are typically attributed to or even expected of a luxury product, such as a gold finish or diamonds for a luxury watch. These help to easily identify a luxury product and to give purchase reassurance. Diverting from typical luxury features of a category needs to be explained with a rationale.

IV.   Purchase reassurance is another key factor in marketing luxury, at least in part justifying the luxury price premium.

V.   Heritage and image are items of utmost importance for luxury products, thus they drive ALV positively by influencing brand equity, providing a purchase rationale and positively influencing the quality perception and experience.

Chapter 8: The Purchase Situation

Objective:
Present the luxury drivers related to the purchase situation

Key aspects:
- Purchase hurdles and uncertainty can stimulate desire
- Limiting distribution to make the purchase situation more unique
- Privacy of shopping
- Waiting times and acquisition rules
- Limiting items
- Make purchase place "invisible"
- "Sucking-up" purchase
- Luxury portfolio considerations
- Mode of acquisition as luxury driver

The purchase situation has an important influence on the perception of luxury. Vice versa, luxury consumers expect certain prerequisites when it comes to purchasing luxury. Table 7 summarizes luxury indicators concerning the purchase situation. They help to create desire, make the offer more unique and relevant. On top they help to make the purchase more special.

Table 7: Luxury Drivers – Quality and Aesthetics

Driver	Luxury Drivers Related to the Purchase Situation
D2.1	Difficulty in acquiring or obtaining an object.
D2.2	Hurdles apart from the price.
D2.3	(Anticipated) uncertainty and surprise at the purchase.
D2.4	Special and selected points of purchase.
D2.5	Brand-exclusive environments or strictly selected multi-brand stores with highest standards of service and specialization.

D2.6	Spectacular shopping experience due to architecture, design and special services.
D2.7	Privacy of shopping.
D2.8	Individualization during the purchase act.
D2.9	Home or web shopping for the most individualized consultation and to keep low profile.
D2.10	Waiting times as part of the unique product experience.
D2.11	Limited available items as part of the unique product experience.
D2.12	Purchase pre-requisitions as part of the product experience: "need to qualify for the right to purchase".
D2.13	Invisibility of the purchase place or luxury access point to create a unique experience.
D2.14	Transformation purchases with the objective to immediately uplift the social status perception.
D2.15	"Complementary purchase": Luxuries may require complementary products or services.
D2.16	Perception of diversity and different offers of one brand.
D2.17	Availability of more expensive limited editions of a line on top of the luxury "base" offer.
D2.18	Availability of "entry-level" items to complement the brand experience.
D2.19	Guilt as negative luxury driver.

Stimulation of Desire

The desire for any good may be stimulated by the difficulty or even the improbability of obtaining the object, unless it is seen as impossible to obtain (Belk et al. 2003). In short, we tend to desire what we cannot have or that we can obtain only with some difficulty.

Given the nature of a luxury item to signal status, it is obvious that it cannot be a product easy to acquire. In other words: a luxury product requires exclusivity (see Dubois et al. 2001).

One important hurdle to achieve exclusivity is of course the high price. Nevertheless, the increasing number of financially affluent people leads to a situation in which price alone is not sufficient as hurdle. Thus, additional difficulties to acquire the product may be needed in order to drive the luxury perception.

O'Curry and Strahilevitz (2001, p.38f) argue that hedonic goods generally provide a specific value, i.e. the value of anticipation: "It is more fun daydreaming about a hedonic experience that involves pleasure than a more utilitarian that does not."

The anticipation utility is the driver of product desire: Anticipation becomes higher the more uncertain an acquisition becomes. Closely related, the likelihood of choosing a hedonic good versus choosing a utilitarian alternative increases with increasing purchase uncertainty (see O'Curry and Strahilevitz 2001). Therefore, some luxury brands are incorporating the element of uncertainty and surprise into their strategy. At the Parisian jeweler JAR "...maybe you'll get a slot that day, maybe not..." (Foroohar 2007, p.48), a fact that attracts a lot of consumers as purchasing becomes a challenge for those who become increasingly bored of "another Pair of Jimmy Choos or a custom-made Bentley..."

Any anticipated purchase uncertainty or anticipated surprise during the purchase, in a sense a purchase hurdle, can make the product more special and more exclusive for some consumers. At the same time we suggest, that a hurdle may also reinforce the signal of expertise due to the fact that someone was able to overcome the difficulty of acquisition. In that sense, the acquisition hurdle may also serve as a further rationale for the luxury price premium.

There are several strategies of setting acquisition hurdles apart from the price. We suggest as important hurdles for luxuries:

- Limiting distribution.
- Setting waiting times until an item is available.
- Limiting the number of items per se.
- Defining strict acquisition rules.
- "Invisibility" of the purchase place.

Limiting Distribution

Limiting distribution may be the most basic hurdle for luxury products. We suggest that it is even a sheer precondition for luxury. For a mass-market product it is important to address the maximum number of the total population by being widely available in all relevant sales points.

Being ubiquitous, mass-market brands avoid substitution by competition at the point of sale.

If a luxury brand used a similar strategy, it would lose exclusivity and appeal, resulting in a significant reduction of ALV. Therefore the principles of purchasing a luxury good seem to be diametrically different from a mass-market product. We suggest that it is important to make any luxury purchase "something special", evoking desire. Among other factors this requires special and limited places for the purchase.

Apart from limiting the distribution points to few top cities per country and within the top cities to the most prestigious shopping streets, some top-level brands go one step further. Louis Vuitton offers a part of the collection only in certain countries or even limited to certain stores. For example, some Louis Vuitton handbags are exclusively sold in Japan and cannot be purchased anywhere else. Prada offers some of their top end items only in very few selected stores.

Limiting the distribution points allows a far better control of the shopping experience. Therefore most luxury brands sell products exclusively in own stores, where competing brands are not available and where the brand image can be best displayed and transported.

Some categories, like luxury watches or jewelry, are typically offered in multi-brand environments; however in those cases normally the distribution is limited to few retailers that match highest standards in terms of ambience, product display and expert advice. Examples are Wempe in New York or Harrods in London. Nonetheless, even in the category of luxury jewelry and watches, some brands are exclusively available in their own stores, such as Tiffany, Mikimoto and Cartier.

Luxury sales points are typically designed as flagship stores. For the most prestigious locations luxury brands even commission leading architects to design the spaces.

In such environments dedicated, specially trained and educated staff can explain the product, the image and history as well as the materials and special craftsmanship in production in much more detail than it would be possible if the product were sold in a multi-brand environment.

Exclusive environments also offer privacy during the purchase situation, allowing separating from the rest of the world and getting undivided attention from the sales staff. Jewelers typically offer special booths or séparées, where products can be experienced in total privacy. We suggest that an exclusive shopping environment strongly adds to the luxury experience and drives ALV.

Privacy also becomes an important factor as some of the world's famous shopping streets like 5th Avenue in New York or Rodeo Drive in Beverly Hills, Los Angeles are becoming more and more filled with tourists instead of luxury buyers. This phenomenon can dramatically decrease the luxury shopping experience. Guinness (2007, online) cites Mario Grauso, president of the group that owns Nina Ricci and Paco Rabanne brands, "It's not the shopping experience anymore. You don't want a busload of tourists out front taking pictures."

Even in a crowded environment some brands manage to maintain privacy of shopping. An example can be found at 420, Rodeo Drive with Bijan. It is an exclusive designer store, even dubbed as the single most expensive store in the world, in which average consumers spend approximately $100,000 per visit according to seeing-stars.com (2007), an internet guide to celebrities and Hollywood. Consequently, given the crowds of estimated 14 million visitors per year on Rodeo Drive (Guinness 2007), Bijan's philosophy is to be the world's only "by appointment only" boutique, which assures exclusivity and privacy of shopping of its client list reaching from heads of state, captains of industry, presidents to kings and emperors (Bijan 2012).

The desire for privacy and individuality is in part driving the trend of online luxury shopping: "...while the rich are clearly willing to pay almost any price for great service, they are also increasingly interested in immediacy and convenience.

As a result, most luxury brands now offer online shopping, including exclusive online-only items. With those, consumers shopping online have the guarantee to purchase highly individual items only. We suggest that also online an ultimate shopping experience needs to be created.

As more and more people visit luxury shopping streets and stores, it's not a surprise that services emerge that allow consultancy and product demonstration in total privacy at home. As Thomas (2007, p.77) describes, "Like queens holding court, many couture clients now receive their dress-makers at home". One reason is that more people who desire more specialized services can afford to fly-in the "vendeuse", the personally assigned expert from the haute couture house that services a client. While more consumers become rich, they seek privacy in purchases to keep a low profile due to their exposed positions: "The couture business has changed because the clientele has changed. Today's couture clients are women working in positions of power and influence" (Thomas 2007, p.77).

Setting Waiting Times

Building up long waiting times until the product is available is another strategy in creating acquisition hurdles and stimulating desire. One of the most famous examples is Hermès' Kelly Bag, which originally was designed for Grace Kelly. Who wants to buy the bag usually needs to wait more than one year until the product is shipped. The waiting time has become part of the fame of the product, and we assume that it would lose a part of its appeal if it were immediately available.

Probably therefore Hermès would not trade-in this sales strategy even in exceptional cases. One of the authors personally knows a case where a waiter accidentally poured red wine over a white Kelly bag in the top restaurant of one of the most prestigious and expensive hotels in Tokyo. The hotel could only calm down the upset owner by offering vouchers for some days of free stay after even the top-management of the hotel was not able to immediately replace the stained bag by a new one, simply due to the long waiting time.

Limiting the Number of Items

Limiting the total number of products available may increase the value of a luxury item in a significant way. This is often the case for top end watches that are only sold in limited editions.

Strict Acquisition Rules

A variation of this strategy is to allow the purchase only if the interested person has a purchase history with the company and is among their top clients. We believe that this drastic limitation strategy sends one of the strongest signals of purchasing power: Owning a product with such a high hurdle unmistakably signals that the owner is part of a very limited circle. The V12 Ferrari Enzo, apart from being limited to 399 plus one (for the Pope) cars, was only sold to previous customers of Ferrari's F40 or F50 models, of which the company was convinced that they would "deserve" to drive such a car and able to handle and appreciate it properly.

One of Patek Philippe's top-end pieces, the Sky Moon tourbillion, is double sided, showing the movements of the stars on one of the watch's faces, and comes at a price of $900,000. The watches are only built on commission, which is accepted only after an interview with the company in Geneva. After approval the waiting time can be up to four years. Willis (2007, online) confirms the strong desire – and thus value – that this policy creates: "For some well-heeled buyers, including the hedge fund crowd, the wait was intolerable: Time [magazine] found buyers dropping $1.2-million on slightly used Sky Moon watches in auctions, in order to avoid the line".

A clear conclusion is that the need to qualify for a purchase due to acquisition rules can be a strong luxury driver in terms of desire stimulation and value perception.

"Invisibility" of the Purchase Place

It might sound weird, but making a point of purchase or a luxury "access point" invisible or at least hard to find, may be another interesting strategy in driving added luxury value. An indicator is that "New York's hippest bars are so low profile they're practically invisible. Persistence – or connections – are required" (Yabroff 2007, p.56), as those bars can not be distinguished from the outside: "Discretion is the watchword when it comes to getting through the (unmarked) doors of these secret Manhattan nightspots, but once inside, you'll be rewarded with swank furnishings, lovingly crafted cocktails, and the discreet thrill of having made it to the inner sanctum."

Rationale is the creation of a totally unique experience with the reassurance of being one of the selected few, who know about the special place and have expertise and status to find and access it.

A variation of this access limitation strategy is represented by closed online communities, which have strict access criteria, so that all members belong to a distinct group of similar interest, income and social status. While those communities are still "visible", e.g. the homepage can be found in the web, they cannot be accessed without recommendation, membership and password.

All activities are exclusive for members and can include exclusive luxury travel offers, private views with top artists, exclusive access to the VIP area of concerts, golf tournaments, etc. The venues stay secret or "invisible" to all non-members.

"Sucking up" Purchase

The 1990 movie "Pretty Woman" shows a specific purchase situation for luxury, the "sucking up" purchase: Richard Gere is cast as successful business man who hires a "companion", played by Julia Roberts, to stay with him for several days. In order to accompany him to exclusive dinners and events, she needs to learn how to choose, buy, and wear the finest of fashion. Mr. Gere takes his new companion to the finest boutiques and instructs the sales clerks to start "sucking up" to make the sale. Ms. Roberts gets all the immediate attention she needs to make the right choices in clothing.

As a result, she is immediately transformed from a "grey mouse" into a society lady. Similar to the situation in the movie, luxuries may be purchased in large amounts or completely outside of the usual experience field with the objective immediately uplift the perceived social status, leading to the requirement of complementary services, such as education.

This situation is not limited exclusively to the "Pretty Woman" constellation. With the number of millionaires rising for example in Asia and the ongoing boom of luxury sales in Russia, there is a soaring number of people who want to adapt their lifestyle in a very brief time frame to their new wealth situation. Young (2007, online) highlights this tendency by citing a luxury executive in Russia: "During the Soviet Union, people didn't have much choice at all. That's why there is still a tendency in Russia for some wealthy people to be overdressed, especially women."

86

The challenge for managing luxury is to service those new clients in an appropriate way, providing the right product portfolio as well as hints and even "education" on how to wear a dress properly, how to drive a sportscar or how to drink a luxury wine.

Luxury Portfolio at the Event of the Purchase

Moe and Fader (2001) outline an important facet of managing luxury, related to its purchase. Their research indicates that hedonic products are often not purchased in a single, isolated way, but rather as part of a portfolio.

For example, a luxury sports car is often the second, third or fourth car of the owner. If it is not driven every day, but on special occasions only, for example on a racing ground, the rather functional boot space will be less important for the purchaser than the offer of additional services with the purchase. Those could be services like granting access to exclusive racetracks or high speed racing trainings with active or retired Formula 1 drivers. For a luxury watch collector, an additional limited edition watch with the prospect of owning an absolutely exclusive piece might be the key reason for purchasing a brand. Hence, the management of the product portfolio and portfolio-related services seem important for luxury goods. Ignoring the portfolio aspect might decrease perceived ALV or might even make an offer irrelevant.

A further portfolio strategy is stretching a luxury brand by offering several different luxury items as part of one brand umbrella. This may also include items of different categories. The benefit for consumers is the opportunity to experience a luxury brand in different situations or across categories. Also it helps to avoid boredom in relation to a brand. Galbraith (2006) concludes that today's luxury consumers even expect a certain degree of diversification.

Luxury brand extensions and portfolios offer an opportunity for consumer segmentation, providing the spirit of the brand to different consumers according to their needs and stages in life and according to their position on the inverse pyramid model. Furthermore, they have the effect of enriching a luxury brand with additional facets. Lane (2001) even suggests that, different to the predominant view that line extensions need to be congruent with the brand, a combination of highly incongruent extensions with repeated advertising might lead to positive product evaluations and higher usage intentions.

The fact that Armani also sells branded flowers and chocolate has therefore the opportunity to enrich the overall brand perception by giving it an edge of unexpected excitement and fun that other brands do not have. Even if incongruent in terms of category or product, we argue that a consistent fit to the brand world is of utmost importance for any portfolio extension.

On the other extreme, portfolio differentiation towards entry level items is typical for a lot of today's luxury brands: Bentley introduced the more accessible Continental models some years ago, Porsche introduced the Cayman, a significantly cheaper alternative to the 911, Bang & Olufsen offers more accessible sound systems, the Beoplay line.

While still being premium and out of reach for most people, those products build an entry point to the brand and offer complementary brand experiences. However, any entry point item that may become perceived as too cheap or too low in terms of quality incorporates the risk of diluting a previously sharper defined luxury positioning.

Therefore, such line extensions may come at a price for brands. Tom Ford states, "The problem today, and we helped to create it, is the idea of democratized luxury. I don't believe that democratized luxury is true luxury any longer" (Newsweek 2007, p.73). During the background research for this paper, the author got to know that even for a relatively exclusive brand like Bentley, some owners of the top-of-the-line model started complaining that too many people own a Bentley. Indeed, in some very affluent neighborhoods two, three or more Bentleys may be spotted recently. This is an obvious risk in terms of perceived exclusivity.

Acquisition Mode

A different aspect of the purchase situation relates to the mode of acquisition. O'Curry and Strahilevitz (2001) found out that hedonic products trigger less feeling of guilt when purchased using windfall money instead of the normal available income. Windfall money could be a bonus or a lottery prize. Furthermore they distilled that the same occurs, when a luxury is not bought for oneself, but as a gift for others.

What is the reason? The feeling of guilt might occur by reflecting about high investments related to luxury, and by uncertainty about reactions of others. Also the perception of frivolity for one's self connected with a luxury purchase might trigger a feeling of guilt. Windfall money is unexpected and not mentally budgeted. Regular income seems mentally accounted for paying the regular bills while extra (bonus, lottery) money can be spent on more luxurious items. Often people feel guilty spending on themselves, but it is OK to buy luxuries as gifts for loved ones.

If the feeling of guilt occurs in a strong way, people might refrain from purchasing at all. Therefore it negatively influences luxury.

A showcase on how to manage potential guilt is Patek Philippe's advertising approach of emphasizing that the true intention of buying their luxury watches is not the ownership by the purchaser. Instead, the ad campaigns highlight that it is an investment for the next generations, who will one day inherit it. Thus, purchasing rationale in the advertising is the role of the product as gift for the next generation, or in other words, as a wise investment. This point of view reduces the risk that the product is seen as frivolous treat for oneself.

Other ways to manage guilt and also to reduce or annualize the high premium of acquiring and maintaining luxury goods, are financing, servicing, leasing or fractional ownership plans. They allow to "rationalize" the purchase: A fractionally owned plane might still have a very similar added luxury value compared to a fully owned plane, however the owner can "excuse" that the plane is used in part only, e.g. for his or her business necessities.

Summary: Luxury Driver – Purchase Situation

In summary, the purchase situation is strongly affecting the added luxury value and the likelihood of the acquisition:

I.   Anticipation is a key driver of desire for a hedonic purchase; it seems especially relevant for luxuries. Anticipation is boosted once the product is difficult to acquire. The minimum purchase hurdle for luxury is limiting the numerical distribution points, usually to few top cities and their top spots with the aim to stimulate desire and thus motivate the purchase.

II. Waiting time, limited editions and setting rules for purchase further increase the exclusivity of a luxury, increasing its added luxury value.

III. Luxury goods are often purchased as part of an individual portfolio, thus the management of the luxury portfolio in terms of consumer segmentation and resulting product offers is decisive for the luxury experience.

IV. Mono-brand stores, often as dedicated flagship stores, allow individually servicing consumers, offering discretion and creating an exclusive brand experience that drives ALV.

V. The mode of acquisition through windfall money or as gift increases the likelihood to buy a luxury. Potential negative luxury effects, such as guilt, may be offset or minimized by those acquisition modes.

Chapter 9: The Consumption Situation

Objective:
Analysis how the consumption situation drives luxury

Key aspects:
- Create products that evoke symbolic relationships
- Consumption premiums and difficulties as luxury drivers
- Unique, not-done-yet experiences
- Individual consumption strategies
- Consumption portfolio opportunities
- Risk of feeling "betrayed"
- Shelter and protection provided by luxury goods
- Social climbing
- Social reference groups

Consuming a luxury impacts the total luxury experience: Luxury consumption can trigger conclusions about the user, which was already indicated in the chapter about the luxury signal. Among others those could be perceptions of exceptional fun, excitement or social protection, e.g. when a beautiful dress and a diamond necklace are worn at a dinner party. The very personal satisfaction of being exceptionally well treated in a luxury resort might even lead to an absolutely unique experience, difficult to repeat or match.

In contrast, a luxury consumption situation may also trigger negative feelings or reactions, such as doubt or guilt, e.g. if the dress does not fit the woman or if the diamonds are seen as "too much" in a context, being negatively commented by the other guests. It can even trigger disappointment and anger when expectations are not met.

On a first glance it might even appear that consuming a luxury is its point of truth. However, there is a watchout as we concluded previously that buying is also very important and that exceptional luxury goods might never be used at all and may even be perceived as pieces of art. But if luxury goods are pieces of art, one could also conclude that watching them or simply heaving them around – observing and admiring instead of using them – is "consuming".

Therefore we conclude that consuming luxury is an important luxury driver. Table 8 provides an overview.

Table 8: Luxury Drivers – Consumption Situation

Driver	Luxury Drivers Related to the Consumption Situation
D3.1	Creating goods that evoke consumers to develop strong symbolic relationships.
D3.2	Premiums of consumption.
D3.3	Familiarity with the category (increasing the likelihood to consume a specific luxury).
D3.4	Expertise on the category (enabling to perform luxury-related tasks).
D3.5	Overcoming consumption hurdles (helping to attribute higher sophistication).
D3.6	Combining acquisition, consumption and maintenance hurdles (further increasing desire and thus leading to higher perceived added luxury value).
D3.7	Not-done-yet experiences.
D3.8	Individual consumption strategies (driving the individual luxury portfolio).
D3.9	Luxury brand-alliances (further enhancing perceived exclusivity of the experience).
D3.10	Collecting (consumption pattern that facilitates luxury consumption).
D3.11	Anticipation or perception of social protection.
D3.12	Uncertainty about consumption ("the best will surely serve").
D3.13	Social climbing.
D3.14	Social reference group's consumption (partly determining the individual luxury consumption).

Experiences and Symbolic Relationships

Belk (1985) has underlined the importance of the experience related to the consumption of a good. His research suggests that experiences become part of the set of possessions of people. Belk (1988) also concludes that consumers may develop symbolic relationships with their possessions. It means that the consumption experience with a product can go much beyond pure utilization: it can have relationship-like characteristics with strong influence on the entire life of people.

This being the case, it becomes an important luxury driver if a brand is able to create products that evoke such symbolic relations. Custom-made jewelry can evoke such symbolic relations upon use: just think of wedding rings.

A symbolic relation may create a very strong bonding between the consumer and the brand as a result of the strong emotional involvement. We expect price sensitivity to be lower as the judgment is mainly made with the heart. During the background research for this paper the authors got to know a striking example from a person with close contacts to the management of Bugatti: All five models of the world's most expensive car, the Bugatti Veyron Pur Sang, have been sold during a single dinner with potential clients. Thus the sale of the most expensive items of a category was done in an emotional situation, outside of the normal context of the clients.

On the other hand, if people develop a strong symbolic relationship, they are also extremely sensitive to the feeling of being betrayed. A previously exclusive brand that stretches its target group too much or that does not perform on the brand's positioning, risks to upset and subsequently lose its top clients. In a sense, the emotional linkage is much stronger with luxury. A luxury brand is rewarded with loyalty when it delivers, but if the consumers feel bad about the brand, the brand will lose them and all their friends.

Symbolic relations can only be created and maintained by repeatedly providing exceptional experiences. Therefore we suggest that the product experience plays an elevated role for luxuries compared with normal goods.

Some Ferrari drivers even worship the brand in such a way that they travel around the world with their cars to participate in especially organized Ferrari races. For them using the Ferrari is seen as performing a very rare and exclusive "sports". Others, who are rather car collectors, might never use the car but enjoy the experience of admiring the sophistication of the car's design in their garage, often even as part of a vast collection of cars.

Premium of Consumption

We have shown that luxuries often imply a significant premium of consumption: the haute-couture dress that not every woman can wear and that may require a special diet and a consequent sports regime, the luxury watch that is not overly precise in telling the time, the luxury sports car that is difficult to drive, to highlight just some. In short, luxuries often require specific knowledge and regimens; they also typically have disadvantages on some purely functionality-related items. As those premiums of consumption increase the exclusivity of the product and make the product more special, we suggest a positive correlation between premium and luxury perception.

Alba and Hutchinson (1987) have done research related to the topic, proposing that consumer knowledge is composed of two components: familiarity and expertise. While familiarity is defined as the sum of accumulated product related experiences, expertise is defined as the ability to perform product-related tasks successfully.

Both aspects are important. The repeated consumption of classy wines will lead successively to more familiarity. I will allow distinguishing taste and aroma. As a result, rare luxury wines can be appreciated and become worthy to drink. In a sense, familiarity should increase the likelihood to consume a specific luxury and can thus be classified as important luxury driver.

The aspect of expertise is a complementary dimension. It would include attributing tastes to several wine brands, grapes and ages, the knowledge of the right serving temperature, the right pouring techniques and the right glasses. Higher expertise is suggested to increase the likelihood of extending the consumption to very rare and very exclusive items, as expertise for the category may be needed to be able to perform tasks in the right way in relation to the luxury.

Consumption premiums of luxury are additional hurdles. Consequently, people who consume luxuries may be perceived as "experts" who have more sophistication. We therefore suggest that a luxury good rewards the consumer by attributing consumption expertise to him or her. This attribution might go as far as suggesting higher education and cultural expertise. Or it may provide expertise to those who are uneducated but want to buy for those who are, e.g. men buying a handbag for a partner.

As a result of being attributed with expertise, consuming a luxury good further enhances the perception of individualism. We therefore suggest that ALV increases with increased attributed expertise. In short, the more sophisticated the consumption, the higher the added luxury value: If someone does not only own a private jet, but also knows how to pilot it, he or she is overcoming one important hurdle. It makes the consumption more exclusive and special.

Special Moments and Not-Done-Yet Experiences

A "not-done-yet" experience by a scarce offer of a physically limited product, even beyond pure exclusivity, may also cause a perceived consumption premium. We suggest that this premium is related to the risk of doing something that has not been experienced before and that is likely not to happen again.

When the authors asked their acquaintances about their "personal luxury" during the background research for this paper, a lot of them answered, "having time for myself". Although we provided a rationale why time is not a luxury per se, these subjective and spontaneous claims suggest that personal, special moments and unique, remarkable experiences – thus the way time is spent – are true luxury drivers. Such a special moment with a distinct experience is, in a sense, an "individualized" experience, in its extreme only available once.

Seeking a unique experience is a clear tendency in terms of consumption. Indicators are increasing numbers of people hiring a personal trainer, a personal shopper or a personal stylist to create a unique, very personal experience. Where does the desire for special experiences, for status and social role-definition end? We suggest that even people who can literally afford whatever they want still seek further differentiation and status.

With an increasing number of billionaires and millionaires worldwide, there is the desire to differentiate even at the top end: Some, like the Oracle founder Larry Ellison, engage in highly visible sports like the America's Cup sailing tournament. Others, like Bill Gates or Warren Buffet, strongly engage in philanthropy, donating billions of dollars to foundations, trying to make a difference for good cause and, seemingly, enjoying this unique luxury.

If you can have anything you want, "the most discreetly fashionable gesture of all, it turns out, is giving it all away. There has been a sharp rise in philanthropic giving among the growing crop of younger financiers and entrepreneurs, often via their own namesake foundations" (Foroohar 2007, p.51).

Consumption Strategies

The consumption situation has a strong influence on the product category choice for a luxury experience. It is obvious that a person who does not play golf is not likely to consume any luxury goods related to golf. Someone who does not drink alcohol will not consume the 1902 Château Latour. On the other hand, an affinity towards a certain category will most probably strongly drive luxury consumption within that category. This explains why some people, for example those with love for nature and gardening, invest in some cases millions of Euros into a collection of Japanese koi fishes for their garden pond. Those findings are consistent with the findings on luxury expertise and familiarity.

We suggest that people tend to consume luxuries as part of a personal "portfolio strategy". Once luxury consumption gets more consistent with a person moving up towards a stage of predominant luxury consumption, ("those who know" in the inverse pyramid model), it is likely that complementary luxury consumption is done.

This is an important implication for the management of luxury: we suggest that it is decisive to understand the individual consumption portfolios of customers in order to offer the right product portfolio. Figure 14 summarizes different individual consumption strategies for luxury.

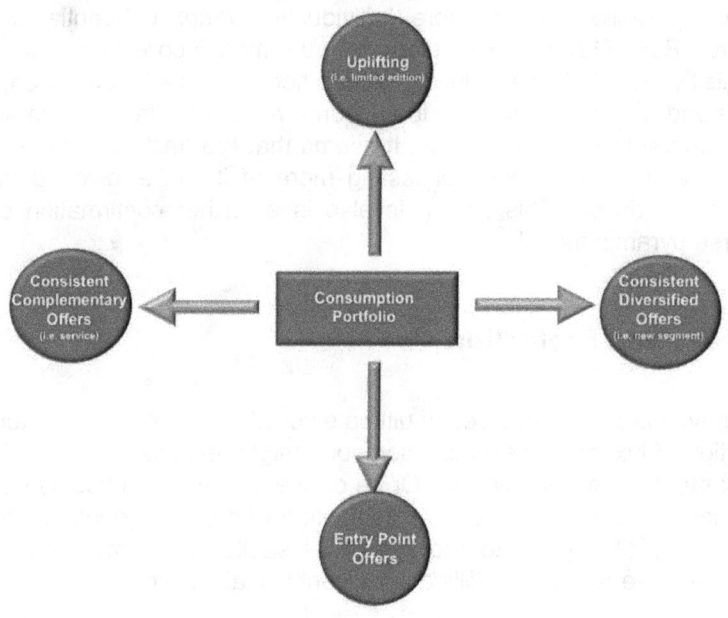

Figure 14: Individual Luxury Consumption Portfolio Strategies

To serve the consumption portfolio aspect, brand-alliances can be particularly interesting to assure the availability of complementary products that one brand alone cannot offer.

The advantage of such alliances is that it offers the best from different brand worlds and brand expertises. A watch from Bentley would have probably little credibility and estimation among watch enthusiasts. Likewise, a car from Breitling would be similarly problematic in terms of credibility and image. However combining both worlds might even create an offer that is more powerful than each world by itself as it has the potential to merge two "legends". If something rare is combined with something else that is similarly rare, it should by definition become something even more exclusive. An indication is that watches of Breitling for Bentley achieve price premiums of factor five to ten compared to the "normal" Breitling watch portfolio.

An important facet of luxury "consumption" in the meaning of admiring is collecting. From a consumer perspective, collecting allows to create a unique portfolio and therefore individually further differentiates from others. Belk (1988, 154) states: "Furthermore, collecting legitimizes acquisitiveness". Once a luxury acquisition is done in one area, it is perceived as being legitimate to consume related luxuries, which should lead in total to more purchases. It seems that the "taste of added luxury value" leads to the desire of tasting more of it, while lowering mental hurdles to do so. This finding is also is a further confirmation of the inverse pyramid model.

Shelter and Protection

We have introduced the idea of ultimate social protection and shelter as a function of luxury. For example someone might feel more attractive using a luxury, despite not being so. Or he or she can signal status by wearing a Patek Philippe wristwatch in combination with casual jeans and t-shirt. The ability of a good to provide social shelter and protection should strongly drive ALV as it fulfills a significant social function.

The second aspect of social shelter is signaling decision quality. In a nutshell, if someone is uncertain what to buy, the best (or most expensive) will surely serve.

Uncertainty could also have the opposite effect, especially if consumers lack knowledge and expertise. We suggest that social shelter will end once others perceive a luxury good as too much, too flashy or not appropriate.

Our general framework is able to explain this: the flashiness would be a moderator, distorting the signal with the result of weakening luxury's added value if other supporting luxuries are not also in place. The distortion of the signal reduces the ability to socially shelter. An example is Versace's colorful men's shirt design used in the 90s that was quite flashy anywhere outside of Miami. On the other hand, if someone – as a signal of social acceptance and admiration – receives repeatedly compliments for an haute-couture dress or a luxury watch, it will probably lead to the perception of shelter and stimulate further luxury consumption.

Luxury as Social Climbing: The Circle of Desire

The consumption of luxury determines loyalty in terms of repurchase, additional purchase or portfolio purchase. Belk et al. (2003) describe the concept of loyalty longing as cycle of desire: if a desire is realized, it is quelled until another object of longing is found, leading to an endless cycle. It explains the development of hypothetical consumer history from consuming prosecco, and then developing from "normal" champagne towards Dom Perignon over time. In a sense, luxury consumption may also influence social climbing, thus social climbing drives luxury consumption. The phenomenon is also a logical result of the proposition on luxury being an "ID card" to distinct social groups. Once someone has climbed up along the social ladder, a "new ID" might be required or seen as appropriate.

Crossland and Smith (2001) showed that goods, which are consumed in public and which are therefore visible for others, are affecting the consumption of others. Luxuries – due to their social uplifting and marker functions – are often goods consumed in public. We suggest that visible luxury consumption therefore stimulates others to follow.

In Japan, where people travel predominantly by train or plane rather than by car, the visibility of luggage is generally higher than in Europe. Therefore Japanese people tend to utilize luxury luggage much more in comparison to people in Europe, according to the author's observation.

An important managerial implication is to influence the consumption situation in a way to increase visibility. This is a delicate task, as too much visibility and exposure is expected to decrease desire.

Summary: Luxury Driver – Consumption

Summarized, the key consumption aspects that drive luxury are:

I.   ALV can be increased by a consumption premium, either due to the need of familiarity and expertise or through the perceived risk caused by a "not- done-yet" experience.

II.   Luxury consumption is influenced by the familiarity and affinity to certain product categories. People are most likely to consume luxury goods in categories that are personally important to them.

III. As luxuries may be often consumed as part of a portfolio, luxury portfolio management is an important managerial task. Portfolio-related consumption may lower potential hurdles to consume additional luxury goods.

IV.   Social shelter is suggested to be a driver of ALV, in its function to provide public protection or improve the decision expertise.

V.   The "cycle of desire" concept suggests that people will move up from one consumption experience to the next. Also, public consumption stimulates others to consume.

Chapter 10: The Cultural and Social Frame

Objective:
Present implications of the cultural and social frame on luxury

Key aspects:
- The role of social relationships
- Image shaping
- Code mimicing
- Negative social effects can limit and boost
- Immoral consumption to break out of a "routine"
- The role of values and norms in regards to luxury
- Social uplifting and downgrading

There might be people who consume whatever they want and totally ignore the social setup around them. However, we suggest that for most people the social frame has an important effect on their luxury consumption behavior. We have distilled that the social frame can be a luxury facilitator, as luxuries may lead to attribution of status, power, attractiveness or expertise. It may also be a limiter, as guilt, envy or fear of loss might decrease the willingness to consume.

Luxuries may influence social relations. They may help to shape a desired image, or they may be a means to follow accepted or even expected codes. The latter becomes clear if someone thinks of the president of a country who would live in a small flat and wear cheap clothes. It would simply not fit the image of someone in power to represent millions of people. Luxury seems to need the "normal" to standout, to be distinguished as something truly special and to be able to differentiate. Therefore, luxury strongly depends on universally accepted codes, values or norms. In this chapter we will distill a set of luxury indicators from the cultural and social frame, summarized in Table 9.

Table 9: Luxury Drivers – Cultural and Social Frame

Driver	Luxury Drivers Related to the Cultural and Social Frame
D4.1	Anticipation of higher attention and more refined service.
D4.2	Facilitation of social relations, leading towards the idealized social destiny.
D4.3	Shaping a desired image.
D4.4	Mimicing the codes of a desired social class.
D4.5	High "luxury reliability" of a brand: permanently perceivably deliver what consumers expect from performance and universally accept.
D4.6	High "luxury validity" of a brand: permanently perceivably send an authentic message.
D4.7	High "luxury compatibility" of a brand: ability to limit negative reactions below a critical threshold.
D4.8	Linkage of a luxury good to culture ("the luxury good becomes part of history")
D4.9	Immoral consumption to break out of monotony of everyday life.
D4.10	Create an image to be at the borderline of reality and provocative: "oversexed, overindulged, underworked, underfed".
D4.11	Prospect of social uplifting, hence the relative downgrading of peers.
D4.12	Challenging the social reference group's perception of social status-quo concerning norms and habits (potential negative driver).
D4.13	Prospect of power to change the perception of reality.
D4.14	Consistency with social values.

Social Relations

Belk (1988) suggests that the ownership of objects may stimulate social interactions. This should be even more the case for luxury goods that transmit social status signals. Adding self-confidence, attractiveness and shelter are beneficial, positive effects of luxury ownership.

If someone shows up in a spectacular Chanel dress and checks in with her Louis Vuitton luggage in a prestigious hotel, signing in with her American Express Centurion card, she can expect to be rated among the top guests. Probably the staff's attention will be higher, service might be a little more refined and she can expect to receive one of the best rooms they have available. We definitely assume that she will get a higher attention and appreciation than a person in a normal, low profile dress, with cheap luggage and having no credit card.

The power of the shelter of luxury in the social context becomes even more obvious if we imagine her to go later that evening to the hotel's restaurant. Whether she laughs repeatedly far too loud, lets her spoon fall down during the dinner or uses the cutlery in the wrong way: all this is likely to be positively ignored by others. If the same would happen to a low-profile person, of whom the social status is not clear and who might therefore be of less financial or reputational interest to the hotel, the reaction would certainly be different. One just imagine the previous example of the stained Kelly bag happening with any unbranded hand bag: the reaction of the hotel would have probably been less attentive.

In short, luxury signals money and money has the power to transform a person – at least in his or her fantasy – to a better person, stronger, with less fears, more charming, wiser, less vulnerable, in a nutshell: more attractive and with more abilities.

Therefore luxury products are objects of desire, of which Belk et al. (2003, p.337) claim that they are "...hoped to facilitate social relations, joining with idealized others, and directing one's social destiny." Luxury is suggested to be as relevant for a sheik as for a UPS driver on an average income, which – from a different angle – underlines the idea of several clusters of luxury consumption that we introduced earlier.

Image Shaping and Code Mimicing

We propose a further social interaction quality of luxury: signaling and shaping a desired image. While opting for a Porsche will probably connect the driver with a sporty, independent, young image, a Mercedes S-Class might connect associations with an elder, reliable person, maybe the head of a corporation.

One dimension of added luxury value of a luxury brand does, therefore, include a person's attempt to shape a desired image through "controlled signals" inline with the brand positioning and heritage. Menkes (2004, p.12) suggests that Ralph Lauren's clothes signal "I have got a house in the Hamptons", while Chanel would stand for "I am sincerely

French and upmarket". By facilitating to play a desired role in the society, we conclude that luxury allows feeling and being like others.

This facet supports the concept of the social marker function as well as the thoughts on managerial implications of the public visibility of luxury consumption in the previous chapter. We call the signaling and shaping of a desired image the "mimetic nature" of luxury, as it allows mimicing.

The mimetic nature adds on top of sending a message on the financial or social power, positioning the owner according to image signals of the brand. We suggest that it is important that customers perceive the positioning signal as authentic. An article on luxury in Businesswire (2004) points out that there is a paradigm shift in luxury away from consumers simply accepting and believing the suggested quality of existing luxury brands (thus simply relying on the brand name or their known attributes) towards the importance of an authentic total brand experience.

It becomes of high relevance that luxury brands really deliver perceivably what they promise and what consumers expect in relation to performance and values. And there is the need to permanently deliver on the expected unique experience: If a luxury sports car brand promises unparalleled acceleration, all their models need to be outstanding also in relative terms to any competitive offer, especially those of non-luxuries.

If Chanel should indeed intend to be the paradigm for a French and upmarket brand, it needs to be extremely consistent and unique in sending an authentic message.

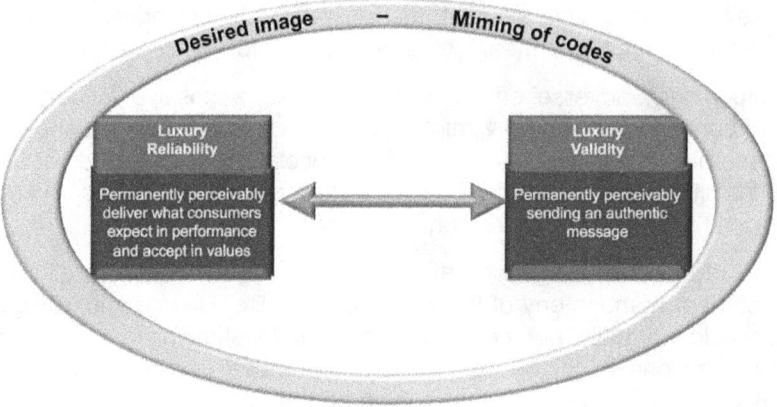

Figure 15: Luxury's Reliability and Validity

Figure 15 summarizes the effect of luxury validity and reliability on the shaping of desired image and mimicing codes. If either validity or reliability are lacking, luxuries are unlikely to be perceived as such and to fulfill their desired social effects.

Negative Social Effects: Limiter or Booster?

Negative social effects and interactions can significantly reduce perceived added luxury value or even completely eliminate it. The most obvious is the evocation of guilt and the resulting need to justify the purchase (see previous chapters and Kivetz and Simonson 2002a).

Often it is not even necessary that there are active negative social reactions: the pure fear of reactions is likely to lead to refrain from buying a luxury, not using it or selling it again. This also happened to fur coats in Europe, which during the 90s almost disappeared as they were seen as immoral.

Luxury managers need to be aware of it and work on reducing negative social pressure. Louis Vuitton as an example is engaging strongly in cultural sponsoring, adding a cultural facet to their products: if a Louis Vuitton product is part of history and culture then it can't be wrong to use it. Also in this context the utilization of celebrities as brand ambassadors may be a means to convince people.

Surprisingly, adverse effects can also have a positive influence on luxury consumption, as they might stimulate desire: Think of dangerous or immoral goods like cigars, super-rich chocolate, luscious foods or a car that for ultimate acceleration burns 80 liters of gasoline each 100km at full speed, like the Bugatti Veyron.

Belk et al. (2003) suggest that those immoral goods are typically used to break out of monotony of the average week life. Hence, a luxury good that would normally not be consumed due to stimulating non-desired social reactions might be consumed on purpose from time to time to break out of the routine. This may also be the $80,000 ring, leased for a special evening, but totally inappropriate for most days of the year.

Tom Ford rebuilt the Gucci brand in the 90s and early 2000s on those principles. Willie (2006, online) confirms that Gucci became a brand with the image of women who live la dolce vita, who are "oversexed, overindulged, underworked and underfed. With past collections including 6in stiletto heels, dental floss bikinis and mini-dresses that more closely resemble belts than skirts, Gucci's clothes have no place in reality, and that's exactly why we adore them. The women who wear them don't need to walk anywhere, or lift a perfectly manicured finger, and these whimsical clients only add to Gucci's mythical status."

A facet of the Gucci approach was the advertising campaign where supermodel Carmen Kaas reveals her pubic hair shaved in form of the letter "G". It was photographed by Mario Testino, unofficially titled "Pubic Enemy" and caused a lot of controversy and public discussion (Vogue 2003). Given the tremendous growth of Gucci during those years, a strategy built on facets of provocation and immorality seems to have potential for luxury if it fits to the brand positioning.

Consequently, the recent stagnation and decline of the brand after the departure of Tom Ford with less provocative brand appearance shows how important authenticity towards a perceived brand image is.

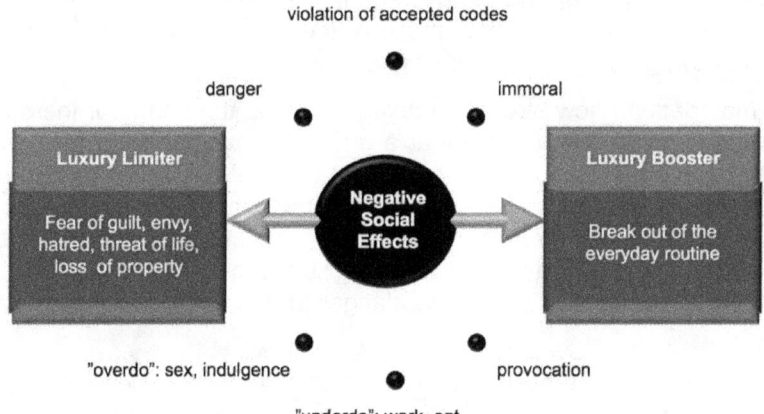

Figure 16: Negative Social Effects as Limiters and Boosters

In certain instances, it can be interesting to load a luxury brand with selected and controlled immoral dimensions in order to make it more special. For a luxury coat it could mean to add on purpose a "forbidden" element, like fur on the inside instead of the outside, so that there is a controlled element of provocation. However, as those dimensions can be limiters and boosters, this might be a fine line to cross (see Figure 16).

Values, Norms and Luxury

As we concluded, it seems that there can't be luxury without the normal. Luxury needs norms, values and yardsticks, which are then exceeded, thus leading to a unique experience. However, as shown, exceeding norms might be a facilitator or a limiter to luxury depending on the amplitude.

Given the power to uplift the image of a person in the social context, a luxury good has an implicit side effect: as a consequence of uplifting the owner or user it relatively "downgrades" the others around the person. One of the most obvious examples is the one of the "neighbor's new car".

If he or she upgrades from an average mid-sized car to a luxury car that clearly exceeds the value and image of the own car, there is an implicit relative downgrading, often resulting in envy.

It may depend how strongly a luxury exceeds the norms of the social reference group. We suggest that a gradual development of increasing luxury consumption over years or a more discreet consumption might be easier to understand and accept by others than an abrupt change or luxury consumption of high visibility. In a sense, luxury consumption challenges the normative and habitual status quo of the surrounding group and thus implies a potential danger for the perceived social setup by others.

In the extreme, the social uplifting power of luxury can become even a danger for the balance of power of a group or society (see Figure 17). Let's imagine a hypothetical quiet mountain village that is mainly living from agriculture and has an established social order with the mayor, the doctor and the owner of the only restaurant seen as the most influential and powerful inhabitants. If suddenly someone builds a luxury house there in order to enjoy the views of the mountain, arriving and leaving on a daily base in a private helicopter and displaying a range of several luxury cars, the perception of the balance of power in the village is most likely to change.

Even if this example is purely hypothetical, it is easy to imagine what might be the one and only topic in the village's bar among the original inhabitants upon of the arrival of the new person displaying all his luxury goods. Probably those talks would be emotional, negative, displaying envy and hatred. At least probably no one in that closed society would be untouched.

Gonzalo Fernández de la Mora, a pioneer of the modern research on envy, provides an explanation for these effects (Müller 2007): According to his research, people feel envy because they perceive the world they are living in by making comparisons. In a nutshell, people identify and classify themselves always in relation to others. Hence, luxury indeed has the power to change the perception of reality.

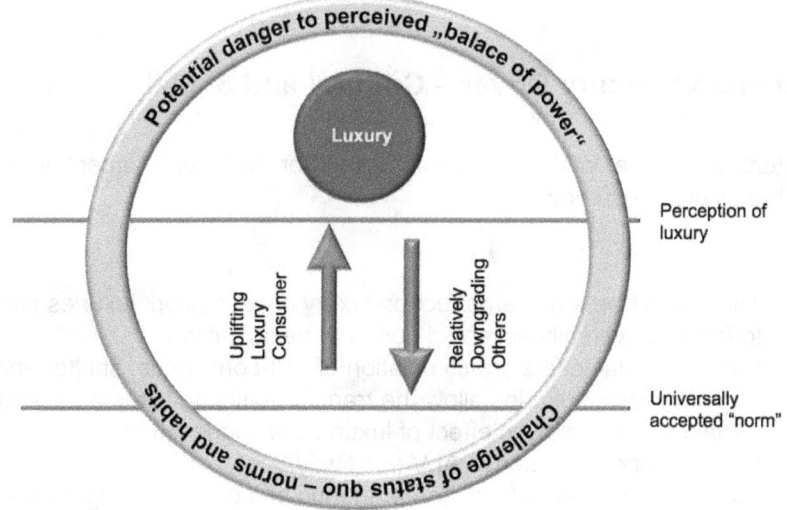

Figure 17: Consequences of Uplifting and Relative Downgrading

The balance between an intended reality change and the adverse effect of challenging or even endangering the balance of power underlines once more that luxuries need to be consistent with social values if their intention is to be sustainable in terms of how they are perceived:

- In terms of the accepted social "balance of power".
- In terms of the accepted level of materialism.
- In terms of the "offensiveness" of the category towards the society.

The importance of social compatibility is increasingly reflected in the way luxury brands communicate. It can be clearly observed as more and more luxury companies place environmental statements on their web sites.

Summary: Luxury Driver – Cultural and Social Frame

Cultural and social influences are important for the luxury perception and for the luxury consumption:

I.   The social frame has an effect on luxury consumption: luxuries need to follow universally accepted codes to be sustainable.
II.   Positive social facets are stimulation of self-confidence, shelter and attractiveness. Luxuries allow the transformation towards a desired social role, the mimetic effect of luxury. We suggest that those positive aspects influence ALV positively.
III. To achieve mimetic effects, an authentic and consistent signal is a precondition.
IV.   Negative facets are adverse social reactions or their anticipation. Adverse behavior by others is suggested to reduce ALV, in some cases ALV might even be eliminated. Obviously, this is likely to limit or even decrease the luxury value.
V.   However, controlled negative aspects, e.g. immorality or provocation, might increase the consumption desire, at least for special moments. Result: boost of luxury value.
VI.   Values and norms are strongly influencing luxury, because social uplifting leads to perceived downgrading by others, thus challenging the social status quo.

Chapter 11: Consumer Segmentation

Objective:
Analyze opportunities of consumer segmentation to drive luxury

Key aspects:
- Segmentation by luxury clusters
- Inverse Pyramid Model offers opportunities for segmentation
- Willingness to pay price premiums
- Consumption portfolio drivers
- Increased distance to luxury weakens the luxury signal
- Intrinsic vs. extrinsic consumption
- Beginner vs. expert

Worldwide there are two major luxury phenomena observable, phenomena that we already covered: The growing number of wealthy people who strive to the exclusive and individualized high-end segment of luxury goods and at the same time the "democratization" of luxury that can be observed almost everywhere. In this context we suggested that the term "luxury" is often even misused and attributed even to extremely ubiquitous and accessible goods of daily consumption.

Some people consume luxury openly, showing-off: a typical element of almost any rap music video. Others instead prefer privacy and discretion. Again others pile up a lot of luxuries for every aspect of life, while the next group might be very selective in luxury consumption.

Table 10: Luxury Drivers – Consumer Segmentation

Driver	Luxury Drivers Related to Consumer Segmentation
D5.1	The individual rank on the inverse pyramid model directly influences the perceived added luxury value of a good (positive or negative moderation).
D5.2	The individual rank on the inverse pyramid model directly influences the willingness to pay high prices.
D5.3	The individual rank on the inverse pyramid model triggers a cluster-distinct expectation on luxury product offers and thus determines luxury consumption.
D5.4	Increasing luxury distance moderates the luxury signal (negative driver).

The latter group might mix original art pieces in their home – say an original Picasso – with cheaper reproductions of other paintings, or mixing expensive furniture with cheap stuff found on a flea market.

All those observations suggest that behavioral or attitudinal aspects of consumer groups, hence segments of luxury consumers, provide a means to further distill luxury drivers, which we summarize in Table 10.

Segmentation by Luxury Clusters

In Chapter 5 we suggested that the consumption pattern of consumers could be described by utilizing the inverse pyramid model: Starting from occasional luxury consumption and finally resulting in very frequent purchase of luxury items with a high degree of individualization. Here one of the key segmentation variables is "purchasing power" as a result of income and wealth and – to a slightly lesser extent – "product knowledge" as a result of expertise and familiarity. The consumption cluster-related segmentation allows a simple prediction of the likelihood with which a person will purchase or consume luxuries: The higher the cluster, the higher is the likelihood of a broad individual luxury portfolio.

The broader and more consistent the individual luxury portfolio, the more consistent the luxury signal becomes. We suggested in the discussion on the general framework of luxury that signal consistency has an effect on the perceived added luxury value in form of positive or negative moderation. Hence, the luxury cluster may influence the perceived added luxury value. In this case, luxury routine and expertise becomes a luxury driver.

This suggestion can help to explain why people who "have it all" still buy more exclusive and more expensive goods. Yes, it is driven by increased purchasing power with increasing wealth. However, it may also be driven by stronger perception of added luxury value due to the higher signal consistency. The $1.4 million Lamborghini Reventón is a good example: "Most of the buyers were men from the United States, some of whom already own a Lamborghini," according to International Herald Tribune (Sep 13, 2007, online).

The individual rank on the inverse pyramid model directly influences the perceived added luxury value of a good (positive or negative moderation). Hence, if added luxury value is perceived to be higher due to higher signal consistency and resulting positive moderation, the willingness to pay high prices is suggested to increase as a direct result (see Figure 18).

The inverse pyramid model also allows deriving specific strategies according to the cluster. Obviously, a "out of luxury" consumer would not be a current target consumer, however – as he or she might become one in future – building brand awareness could be a strategy. In the "occasional" luxury cluster, a luxury brand can mainly stimulate desire. It is quite difficult to actively steer from a company perspective. Maybe someone just starts with very few luxuries, but these will be probably lower cost luxuries, e.g. a handbag and not a car. At this limited and selective consumption stage, further luxury brand awareness building is probably the best strategy.

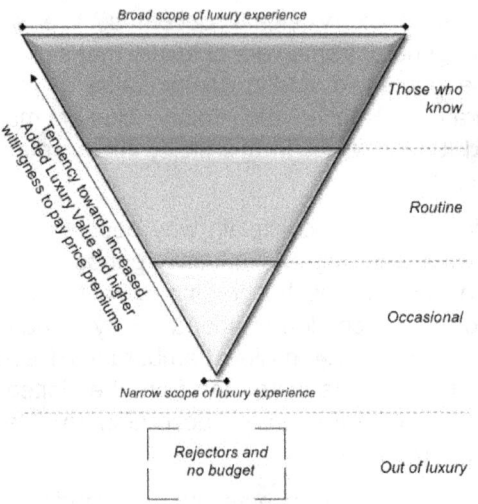

Figure 18: Inverse Pyramid Model and Luxury Value / Luxury Pricing

Building a comprehensive portfolio offer or building luxury brand-alliances can profitably service a more advanced luxury consumer, who buys luxuries regularly.

A routine luxury consumer would probably require an individual top-notch servicing and quality due to his or her very advanced and vast expertise. Those clients, along with their high available wealth, are also likely to demand a broader product portfolio of extremely rare and expensive goods.

This can be the opposite of someone of "those who know". If he or she buys a brand because it is highly individual and because it is able to craft products exactly to the individual needs, a large portfolio, open to a lot of other consumers, can be a fatal mistake. As those consumers are also believed to have very strong symbolic relations to their highly individualized goods, they will most probably not forgive if the brand becomes too ubiquitous.

114

Segmentation by Luxury Distance

Dubois et al. (2005) suggest a further segmentation approach according to proximity or distance towards luxury (see Chapter 1). One of the differences to our segmentation model of the inverse pyramid is that they rely on subjective attitudes and statements of consumers.

Attitudes and behaviors should be a very strong driver of luxury consumption: Someone who does not buy luxuries as a general rule will definitely steer his or her behavior to a large extend independent of perceived added luxury value. However, our general framework suggests that even a rejecter of luxury is prone to the effects of the luxury signal, even if the signal may be perceived in a moderated and weaker way.

Let's look at a rationale: If we compare the perception of added luxury value with the perception of a color, both are a result of a stimulus. One might not like a red color, but the signal will still be perceivable and be processed as red. Similar, one might not like a luxury, however we suggest that the luxury signal will still be perceivable and evoke the processing of status information.

Segmentation by Intrinsic or Extrinsic Consumption

Logic suggests that luxury consumers can be further clustered into two opposite groups, the intrinsically oriented who predominantly purchase for themselves and the extrinsically oriented, who purchase mainly to impress others. In short, either "people who know" or "people who show". Of course, in reality there will be a continuum between both extremes, however we will look at both ends.

Whether people know or show, we suggest that the underlying luxury principles and motivations remain similar. Rationale is that – while this seems logic for extrinsic consumption – also members of the intrinsic cluster will most likely feel more attractive, sheltered and "expert", even if they consume by and for themselves. This can be easily explained by our proposition that a luxury signals status to the owner, too, and not only towards others. Hence, as a general luxury driver, the tendency to consume rather intrinsically or extrinsically should not be of significant influence.

We suggest that the key differences between both are the selection of the products and brands as well as the situation of consumption.

A member of the extrinsic cluster will probably focus more on luxury goods with a high awareness among peers, which also trigger a high desire among others. He or she would probably focus the consumption on goods, which can be shown outside and have a high visibility, such as wristwatches, handbags, jewelry, fur, cars or boats. A rather intrinsically motivated person would either consume the same products discreetly in privacy or focus on products that are less visible to the outside world.

This segmentation leads to the managerial implication to choose on which item to communicate to members of each group. For a luxury car one option could be to highlight the rather intrinsic functions (the wood finish of a car interior, the comfort of a electrical footrest in the back of a limousine, etc.) or rather extrinsic product functions (the exterior design of a car, the "head-turning factor", etc.).

Segmentation by Being Beginner or Expert

A beginner to luxury will surely show a different behavioral and attitudinal footprint compared to an expert. This was dramatized by our example from the movie "Pretty Woman" when we discussed uneducated consumption and furthermore during the discussion of segmentation by luxury clusters. Luxuries are often rather difficult to consume and thus require expertise. A beginner might therefore rather show the tendency to refrain from consuming luxury goods that are too far away from own areas of knowledge.

While a novice in the area of collecting wristwatches could buy three or more watches at once, it is more likely that he or she would rather enter stepwise to the new field and seek assistance and advice from experts. In this phase it is also unlikely that he or she purchases a lot of complementary goods around a luxury.

With growing expertise however, we expect a clear shift to complementary luxury consumption, a phenomena that we assessed with luxury drivers like "familiarity" (driver D3.3), "category expertise" (driver

D3.4) "individual consumption strategies" (driver D3.9), "collecting" (driver D3.10).

On a first view, beginners of a category might seem to have a higher willingness to pay price premiums due to the added luxury value from a not-done-yet experience. However, this is likely to be offset by the added luxury value created by signal consistency, e.g. by the third, fourth or fifth car in a collection. We therefore suggest that it is not clear whether price sensitivity of a beginner would be higher or lower compared to an expert and assuming similar wealth and spending power.

Also increased expertise offers further means of personal differentiation from others, as described as personality trait in the ultimate stage of luxury consumption: People who discover very rare products and objects or have products crafted individually for them, may pay even almost absurd amounts of money, e.g. by acquiring paintings for €100 million and above.

Thus, we suggest that segmentation by beginner versus expert has an influence on luxury consumption. However it does not lead to additional luxury drivers besides the ones already identified in previous chapters.

Summary: Luxury Driver – Segmentation

The perception of luxury is influenced by consumer segmentation:

I. Perceived added-luxury value, the willingness to pay price premiums and the consumed product portfolio may be influenced by the individual rank on the inverse pyramid model.
II. Increasing distance towards luxury, hence the subjective importance rating towards luxury acts as moderating factor on the perception of the luxury signal.

In contrast, being a beginner or expert seems to be of less importance for dissecting additional luxury drivers besides the ones discussed in previous chapters.

The tendency to consume rather intrinsically or extrinsically seems not to be a luxury driver per se, but rather an important influencing variable for the category of consumption and the management of luxury goods.

Chapter 12: Brand and Product Awareness

Objective:
Dissect brand awareness aspects as luxury drivers

Key aspects:
- Unique context provided by brands
- Awareness among peers
- Attention to detail
- Creating and maintaining a legend
- Superiority
- High price point
- Create a universally shared belief

The awareness of a brand is critical for the luxury perception. As we have elaborated, a luxury brand does not need to be known by everyone. However, the target group and the peers should know it. Similarly, materials, performance, heritage are important luxury facets, which need awareness in order to signal status. Table 11 summarizes luxury drivers related to brand and product awareness.

Table 11: Luxury Drivers – Brand and Product Awareness

Driver	Luxury Drivers Related to Brand and Product Awareness
D6.1	Brand equity.
D6.2	Awareness among peers (universally shared belief that a product is a luxury).
D6.3	Attention to every detail of luxury along the complete value chain (creating a universally shared awareness and belief that a product is a luxury).
D6.4	Ability to keep the brand "hot".
D6.5	Ability to keeping the initial legend "alive".
D6.6	Creating awareness of superiority also by being overly expensive.

Brand Equity

Brands play an important role in luxury: Most brands try to create and provide a unique, surprising context, which is interesting enough to attract people and be discussed, and then linking the brand to the context.

Of course, already the isolated awareness of materials and special crafting techniques, like gold finish or diamonds alone might be able to evoke the notion of luxury, even without any assumed brand awareness. This would be typical for jewelry, which normally shines stronger through the way it is crafted and through its diamonds and other precious stones rather than necessarily through the brand (see Luxury Driver D1.2 "rare and expensive materials").

However, the link of special crafting and rare materials with brand equity and brand heritage may help to fully exploit the luxury potential. Thus, luxury brand equity, the quantified sum of the perceived and relevant brand values, becomes a key luxury driver:

Brand and Product Awareness Among Peers

It is obvious that the "luxury signal" of an expensive brand will only work if others than the owner know the brand and its exclusivity.

Therefore it's all about awareness among the peers and the reference group when it comes to luxury. In a sense, it is of utmost importance, that there is a universally shared belief that a specific good is indeed a luxury. This is driven by awareness of brand, items, elements, etc. perceived by both: by the owner and by the peers.

The Lexus brand, a best selling Japanese luxury car brand in the USA, has still a low awareness in Europe, and thus was so far not able to evoke aspiration among most European consumers. Again, imagine the effect on the social status if you spent the equivalent of €100,000 on a Lexus in Germany while your neighbor confuses it with an average mid-priced Toyota. This might change dramatically over the next years, as Lexus is positioning itself to be the pioneer in hybrid technology. With strongly shifting consumer preferences towards low-emission vehicles, the awareness on specific unique sales propositions (USP) "hybrid technology" and "ultimate comfort" might skyrocket brand equity and awareness among a larger audience.

Although there do not seem to be many publications or research projects linking the need of awareness to luxury perception, we suggest that awareness is a necessary luxury factor. We also suggest that awareness has a diametrically different role in the marketing for luxury than in the marketing for any non-luxury item.

In a non-luxury marketing setting, the target groups for awareness building are potential purchasers and consumers. We suggest that the rules of awareness building are significantly more complex in a luxury setting: On one hand, awareness has to be generated among the purchase and consumption target. So far this is similar to normal marketing.

On top, luxury typically requires generating additional awareness among potential non-users on a similar social level compared to the potential purchaser. The rationale is that only awareness among others, to whom a social separation and uplifting should subconsciously or consciously be achieved, will enable the luxury to fulfill the objective by delivering additional luxury value.

When the product is part of a consumption portfolio, even awareness along the entire value chain needs to be carefully managed.

Constantly Fueling the Legend

The elevated requirement for awareness outside of the core target group suggests that luxury products require specific marketing management skills and techniques compared to normal products or brands. It is key to be able to always keep the brand "hot", keep the buzz going and constantly adding desire and surprise. This may contrast with the perception of some small, specialized luxury houses, often run by the founder and building products in a very individualized way. Those houses – shoemakers, some high end audio manufacturers, top-notch wine yards, etc. – often seem to be more focused – also in terms of their internal organization – on the product development process than on marketing. However, not focusing on the marketing side including competitors and consumers and thus not "managing the buzz", puts the sustainability of a luxury business at risk.

A nightmare scenario is the one of becoming suddenly banal by losing appeal and aspiration. Pierre Cardin is a paradigm, since he lost control over too many licenses that still had his name, but did not share the same aspiration and positioning of the original Cardin brand (Gumbel 2007a).

We also suggest that the heritage of the brand – hence its initial legend and origin – needs to be constantly substantiated, because it is usually the original source of its luxury value. This includes the reassurance of awareness of the brand heritage and its history as well as its image, intensifying the identification with the brand and additionally deepening the aspiration level. Not surprisingly most luxury brands emphasize their historical roots.

In a nutshell, a driver of luxury is the ability of a brand to constantly fuel the initial legend of the brand, thus keeping it up to date.

Creating Superiority

In this context, the awareness of a brand's special expertise with materials and extraordinary craftsmanship provides an all-important pillar to separate luxury products from others. If people would not believe that the leather trims of a Rolls-Royce or Bentley dramatically differ from the leather interiors of any other car, a lot of fascination would presumably be lost.

Similarly, creating awareness of extraordinary product features is important to position a brand into a luxury context. This includes creating awareness on the superiority versus other brands. Therefore it is important for a luxury brand to have a clearly perceivable price point in an area that is understood by consumers as luxurious for a specific category. The pricing sets a clear superiority signal. If a brand manages to communicate this top-end price positioning directly or indirectly, it strongly supports its overall superiority statement.

A way to communicate a superior price point indirectly is utilized by the Bijan brand at their Rodeo Drive boutique. Typically one out of their collection of luxury cars, which includes a Mercedes SLR McLaren and – one may say of course – a Bugatti Veyron, is parked outside the boutique, thus signaling that his boutique is indeed expensive.

Figure 19: Awareness as Luxury Driver

123

Summary: Luxury Driver – Awareness

In summary, a luxury good needs awareness to be able to generate added luxury value. Conceptualized as shown in Figure 19, awareness among buyers (or users) of the luxury brand and among their peers has to be built.

It includes awareness of brand equity and superiority and it is additionally comprised of the ability to keep the brand "hot" and the image "alive".

For the management of luxury it is important to pay extraordinary attention to every detail of a luxury along every aspect of the value chain. The result is a universally shared belief that a brand or product is a luxury.

Chapter 13: Take-away from Luxury Drivers

Objective:
What is the take-away from the luxury driver analysis?

Key aspects:
- Multidimensional set of drivers provided (76 drivers identified)
- Key dimensions: quality, purchase and consumption, social frame, consumer segments and awareness
- Typically, only a subset of drivers apply to one individual brand or item

---

The starting point for the driver analysis has been the suggestion that several aspects are able to influence the perception of luxuriousness of a brand or product. We presented this as important in understanding and managing luxury.

Probably no luxury product will touch all drivers at the same time. It is much more likely that each luxury comprises of a distinct and smaller sub-set out of those 76 drivers. Nevertheless, some drivers will be more predominant than others. We have shown for example, that consistency with social values is a key precondition for most luxuries.

It is also possible that some of the drivers can be connected to non-luxuries, too, if we look at them in an isolated way. The facilitation of social relations (D4.2) could be such a driver, because social relations can definitely also be facilitated by non-luxuries, like by a dating agency. However, we suggest that those drivers are relevant in the context of luxury, especially if they appear not in an isolated way, but as part of a set of luxury drivers.

We furthermore suggest that the drivers can be grouped to several factors. For example, both, individualization (D1.1) and rare materials (D1.2) increase the uniqueness of a product. Uniqueness could therefore be a factor comprised of individualization and rare materials, among others.

Chapter 14: Luxury Pricing and Income Elasticity

Objective:
Provide insights on luxury pricing and income elasticity

Key aspects:
- Luxuries are sub-clusters of categories (top-tier of pricing)
- High importance to consumers who purchase and consume luxury
- Absolute price points vs. cross-reference
- Price = ultimate factor in assessing what is luxury
- Strategic Triangle of Luxury
- Income Elasticity Matrix
- Mental accounting
- Luxury as investment

Superficially, the pricing dimension seems to be a quite easy and clear one when it comes to luxury: luxuries are expensive, often overly expensive, marking the top-tier of each product category.

This implies that luxuries are powerful sub-clusters of product categories, receiving their power by meaning a lot to the people buying and utilizing them.

A second view reveals that luxury pricing is much more complex. First, some categories might lack a strong absolute price differentiation of product offers within the category. In this case it can be difficult if not impossible to distinct some goods clearly as luxuries. Even if a premium toilet paper might have 20 times or more the price of the most basic paper, it is more than questionable if it would be perceived as luxury by staying in a very accessible price range of let's say under $5.

Second, categories itself will clearly compete with each other in terms of being perceived as luxury. For a lot of people, even the cheapest private jet would be perceived as luxury as the entry price for the category is not affordable at all for most, while the most expensive toilet paper currently available might still be accessible for basically everyone.

Dubois et al. (2001) argue that luxury price perception is established either on the basis of the absolute value, hence the absolute price tag, or via cross-reference by comparison to non-luxuries. As a result of the examples above, we suggest that in most cases both aspects, the absolute and the relative price, will be taken into account in evaluating a luxury. It is obvious that knowing that a necklace costs $10 million will make it more attractive and desirable compared to one costing $1,000, independent of how beautiful it might be in absolute terms.

We suggest that the price will often be the ultimate factor from a consumer perspective in evaluating what is luxury or not. Once the price is perceived and processed by the consumers, all other key influencing factors, the added luxury value drivers, are rather confirmatory measures. If they are inline with the absolute price the luxury product will be sold, assuming there are people who can afford it. If the added luxury value is perceived as lower, the product won't sell.

This is visualized in Figure 20, the luxury's strategic triangle, based on the ideas of Ohmae (1982, p.91ff). If we assume to offer a hypothetical luxury product, we need to make sure that the added luxury value we create – hence the perceived value of the mix of product heritage, quality, performance, social shelter, and so on – divided by the luxury premium we charge – hence the price premium exceeding the highest price of 99% of the products of a category, thus the non-luxuries – will outperform competing offers towards the same consumer segment. In this case we produce a competitive advantage, the luxury preference.

If added luxury value is not enough to substantiate the luxury premium, we expect that the product will fail in the market, at least in a mid- or long-term time perspective, due to lacking luxury preference within the target segment.

This underlines that price is a fundamental luxury factor, reaching far beyond the purchase hurdle as an exclusivity and desire driver. It has two key roles: First, being the absolute and relative reference point transparent for the social reference group. Second, it is the monetary measure of the total value of the luxury good in terms of the sum of its functional, hedonic and added luxury values.

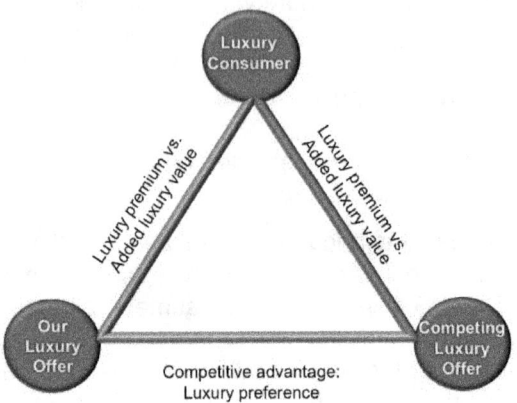

Figure 20: Strategic Triangle of Luxury
Own visualization based on the 3Cs (Ohmae 1982, p.92)

Thus, managing luxury pricing is extremely important and delicate: "One of the worst mistakes a seller can make: marking down. 'If a product is priced too low, it will have the reverse affect on the emotions,'" a pricing consultant is cited by Lindner (2008, online). Underpriced luxury is signaling a too low added luxury value.

What does this mean for income and price elasticity? How will changes in available income and changes in price affect the quantities a luxury brand is able to sell?

The research status quo suggests that income elasticity of luxury should be above 1, as a higher available budget should increase the likelihood of acquiring a luxury (Dubois and Duquesne 1993, Encyclopaedia Britannica 2006). It is also inline with our argumentation on the existence of clusters of luxury consumption depending on increased available wealth. Statistics by Merrill Lynch also confirm this view. According to those, luxury sales increase with the growth of the wealthy class in Russia, China and India, with the result that by 2014 those countries are expected to generate 32 percent of luxury sales (Forden, 2006). Hence, there is a clear correlation between available wealth and luxury consumption.

Additionally, we have shown that unexpected or additional income sources, such as windfall money due to bonuses or lottery wins, additionally facilitate luxury consumption from a psychological viewpoint. Therefore not only long-term increments of wealth and income, but also short-term positive changes should strongly drive luxury consumption.

The same logic should apply for a continuous drop in income or wealth. A billionaire who loses all his wealth due to unfortunate stock speculation and who does not have the prospect to reacquire wealth again in a foreseeable time will not be able to acquire a luxury car or luxury plane anymore.

However, we suggest that a short-term drop in income, such as through a recession or an exceptional year in which no bonus is paid, would not reduce luxury spending to the same extend, leading to an income elasticity below 1 for this case. Luxuries are therefore, as we propose, more stable to short-term negative income changes than non-luxuries. This can be translated to lower price sensitivity for luxuries.

The rationale behind this proposition is the role of luxury satisfying a need and its ability to define or shape the personality of a person. Therefore it is unlikely that consumers will change their purchase strategy due to a short-term downfall in income. Given the significant added luxury value of a luxury good, a fractional change of prices should also not affect luxuries to the same extent as non-luxuries.

This assumption of short-term decrease of sensitivity for income losses, hence lower price sensitivity, is consistent with findings of Chien et al. (2001). They concluded that shoppers tend to show some consistency of price sensitivity across categories. For any premium priced brand this leads to the tendency to be included in the purchase basket with other premium priced brands. Hence, if consumers buy predominantly premium or luxury, this pattern does not change immediately. Also Wakefield and Inman (2003) indicate that social and hedonic consumption decreases price sensitivity compared to non-social consumption.

Concluding, we propose that income elasticity for luxury goods is above 1 for increases of income and wealth (long-term and short-term) as well as a long-term decrease of income and wealth. For a short-term decrease, e.g. through a recession, we suggest elasticity less than 1 (see Figure 21).

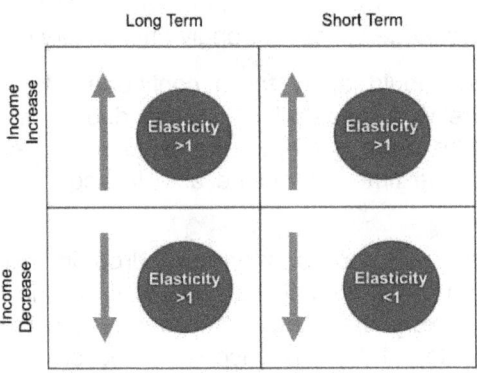

Figure 21: Income Elasticity Matrix for Luxury

In a nutshell, a luxury may not be overly income sensitive for short-term negative deviations. However as, on the other hand, one may need the cash to afford it, luxuries may also not be as price sensitive as non-luxuries.

The latter proposition has an additional rationale in the drivers of added luxury value discussed in the previous chapters: Given the importance of luxury brands for consumers, including heritage and legend, loyalty should be higher compared with non-luxuries. This may result in less perceived competition due to a narrower relevant set and less price sensitivity.

An interesting pricing facet for luxury goods is the concept of mental accounting (see Krivetz 1995). If a luxury is bought rather as investment than as something to be simply consumed, the tendency to spend money on it increases: A drawing of Picasso is more likely to be acquired if it is mentally accounted for as investment and not as a purchase for fun or pure pleasure. In this case, the purchase is rationalized, the negative effects are mentally reduced and the willingness to spend is increased. This concept is important for the management of luxury.

Another facet of mental accounting, reducing price sensitivity, is separating as much as possible the purchase situation from the consumption situation. This may reduce the perceived cost (Krivetz 1995). Think as an example of purchasing several bottles of wine in a box or several Cuban cigars at once, then consuming from time to time. With a separation of purchase from consumption, the likelihood may increase that from time to time a connoisseur will enjoy an expensive bottle of wine or an aficionado will smoke a Cohiba.

Chapter 15: Model of Luxury

Objective:
Provide a comprehensive model of luxury

Key aspects:
- Base for model = general framework of luxury
- Luxury signal triggers added luxury value
- Moderators can strengthen or weaken signal
- Set of indicators of antecedents of luxury
- Set of indicators of added luxury value
- Structural Model of Luxury and validation of research statements
- Additional attitude-based luxury definition
- Implications for luxury managers

Luxury Drivers and Framework

The general framework of luxury, which we developed in Chapter 4 (see Figure 9), is the central base for our model of luxury. We proposed a structure consisting of preconditions for luxury that lead to the classification of a good being a luxury, followed by a luxury signal emitted by the luxury, finally leading to the perceived added luxury value, hence the social status effect. We also suggested that moderators could strengthen or weaken the signal.

How can this framework be "filled" with content to make it measurable? Let's start with the antecedents of luxury, its preconditions. In our luxury driver analysis we have extensively dissected and assessed facets that drive luxury. We concluded for example the factor of "uniqueness" to be a driving force in the perception of luxury. Another driver was "craftsmanship" which could translate in an extraordinary experience in making a product. Usually luxuries are sold in dedicated "flagship stores", an indicator for the importance of having an extraordinary experience in selling a product.

To measure the antecedents of luxury, we therefore need to factor all relevant luxury drivers that build a precondition to few measurable indicators. For each indicator we then need to identify a measurement system that allows identifying its role in explaining luxury.

The central concept of our model is the existence of a luxury signal that leads to perceivable added luxury value. We therefore need to identify a set of key indicators for added luxury value, too. We will dissect this set mainly by utilizing our proposed battery of decoded "hidden" aspects of luxury (see Figure 10), which were further deepened in the discussion on luxury drivers.

It shows that the luxury framework and the luxury drivers are strongly interconnected. The luxury drivers build the base to distill measurable indicators, which will allow assessing and confirming the luxury model.

Indicators of Luxury – Luxury Antecedents and Added Luxury Value

We propose eight indicators for luxury antecedents, as summarized in Table 12. Those indicators allow factoring the key luxury drivers into fewer subclusters that can be measured.

We suggest that all indicators are positively correlated with the perception of a good being a luxury. Hence, the more consistently the indicators can be measured with high scores, the more a good is perceived as luxury.

Someone can only sell a dream if there is a buyer. We suggested that people buying luxury are spending the premiums to a large extend in exchange for the perceived added luxury value, a result of the luxury status signal. In addition to the ten items derived from the set of hidden aspects of luxury of Figure 9, we suggest to include also unique experiences and the aspect of triggering envy as luxury indicators. Table 13 provides an overview of the ALV drivers.

We suggest that the indicators are positively correlated with added luxury value, hence the higher their measure, the more added luxury value is expected. Indicator 12, however, will only be positively correlated with added luxury value if the luxury is universally accepted and consistent with social values.

After identifying key indicators, we needed to omit some due to interdependencies. As an example, the indicators "enhancing social status" and "signaling financial power" should have a very strong interdependency, as social status is very often a result of wealth and the ability to consume. Thus, for the model, we took out indicators to reduce interdependencies.

Langer & Heil (2013) provides more detail on the indicators and measures taken to reduce interdependencies.

Table 12: Indicators of Luxury-Antecedents

Indicator	Related Luxury Drivers (selection)
IA.1 Rare & Unique	» Individualization (product and through purchase act). » Rare materials. » Aesthetics of refinement, excitement, class, style, sophistication. » Top-in-class experience. » Clear connection to an event, a purchase history, a person. » Difficulty in acquiring or obtaining an object. » Waiting times as part of the unique product experience. » Limited available items. » Purchase pre-requisitions (e.g. qualify for purchase).
IA.2 Experience in Making and Selling	» Utilization of highly specialized items that very few experts manage to build and service. » Crafting a good to potentially become a piece of art. » Heritage and image: luxuries have a story or even a legend. » Uncertainty and surprise at the purchase. » Special and selected points of purchase. » Privacy of shopping.
IA.3 High Quality	» Highly refined and carefully designed packaging. » Strict rules and codes for every detail of the aesthetics. » Top-in-class performance in its specific expertise area. » Perceived consistency in terms of superior quality.
IA.4 Difficult to Consume	» Premiums of consumption, consumption hurdles. » Need of familiarity and/or expertise. » Not-done-yet experience.
IA.5 Overly Expensive	» High absolute and relative price point. » Creating awareness of superiority, also by being overly expensive.
IA.6 Consistent with Social Values	» Guilt as negative luxury driver. » Social reference group's consumption habits. » Balance of power of a group or society.
IA.7 Universally Accepted	» Category or brand universally accepted to be able to evoke desires, dreams and aspirations. » Ability to keep the initial legend "alive", to keep the brand "hot".
IA.8 Awareness of Brand, Materials, Items	» Strong brand equity. » Utilization of brand logos. » Materials connected to "luxury world": e.g. gold, leather.

Table 13: Indicators for Added Luxury Value

Indicator	Related Luxury Drivers (selection)
IALV.1 Protects in Public (Public Shelter)	» Shaping of a desired image. » Anticipation of social protection.
IALV.2 Enhances Social Status	» Mimicing the codes of a desired social class. » Facilitation of social relations. » Social climbing.
IALV.3 Signals Financial Power	» Social uplifting implying relative downgrading of peers. » Sucking-up purchase.
IALV4 Signals Expertise and Sophistication	» Ability to overcome consumption hurdles. » Celebrities, royals and experts use the product.
IALV.5 Enhances Self-Esteem	» Power to change the perception of reality.
IALV.6 Enhances Attractiveness	» Consistency of context of purchase and usage. » Symbolic relationships with luxury goods.
IALV.7 Facilitates New Experiences	» Break out of monotony of everyday life.
IALV.8 Signals High Decision Quality	» Buying a product of top-notch craftsmanship.
IALV.9 Enhances Individualism	» Be at the borderline of reality and provocative. » Shopping in a "private" environment. » Result of limited availability. » Being perceived as one of a kind.
IALV.10 Provides Ultimate Treat	» Symbolic relationships. » Top-in-class performance.
IALV.11 Provides Unique Experience	» Stimulation of higher attention and more refined service. » Top-in-class product experience. » Individualized to own needs and preferences. » Spectacular shopping experience.
IALV.12 Triggers Envy (Relative Downgrading)	» Potential danger to the balance of power of a group or society. » Challenges the perception of social status quo. » Luxury compatibility.

From a Framework to a Model of Luxury

The combination of our general framework of luxury with the indicators for luxury antecedents and added luxury value is leading to our proposition of a model for luxury as shown in Figure 22. In a nutshell, the antecedents describe the input factors for luxury, the effects the output factors. The sum of the perceived value of the output factors builds in total the added luxury value.

We include the sender as well as the purchase and consumption situations. The sender should be included due to our proposition on signal consistency. The purchase situation will influence the signal clarity, e.g. just imagine a luxury good sold at a discount price in a low-end department store. The same goes for the consumption situation: A 15m-yacht, parked in a marina among 50m-yachts will trigger a different perception than a 15m-yacht among small boats.

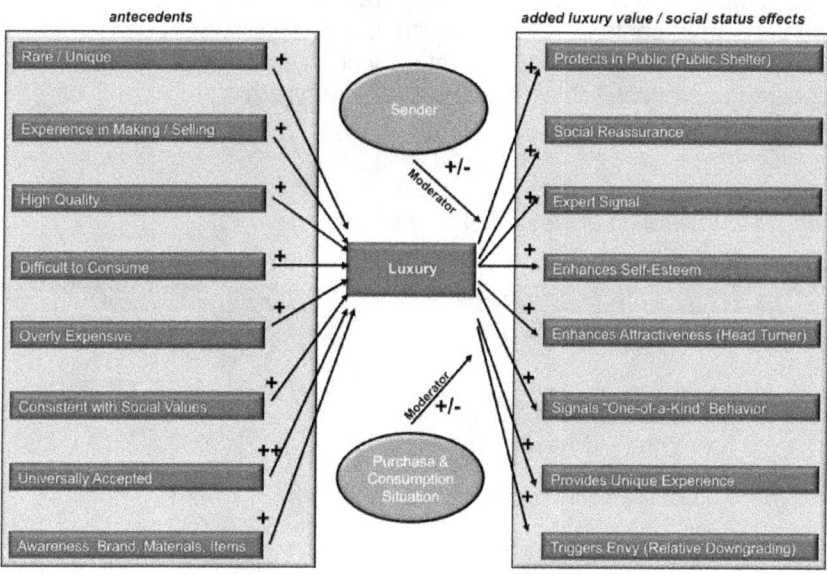

Figure 22: Model of Luxury

We suggest that all indicators in the model correlate positively. However, the indicator "universally accepted" should have the highest effect on the luxury construct. This is because only a good that is unanimously accepted within a social group can be clearly identified as luxury by most of its members.

The indicators with which we describe the construct of luxury and its effects are variables that are not directly measurable. Reason is that they are unobservable without any additional tool. This becomes obvious if we just take the indicator "rare / unique" as an example: The number of items in a given category that would still be classified as "rare" and "unique" surely depends on the category and on individual views. It is important, however, that there is not one single measure that unanimously measures "rare". Therefore this indicator, similar to all others distilled above, is a sub-construct that needs to be measured with a related sub-set of observable items. We measured the indicators with several questions and identified their correlation in order to test the model.

An empirical study validated luxury framework and model in terms of structure and content. The research statements were confirmed and substantiated utilizing several statistical methods in a systematic research approach (Table 14 provides an overview).

Table 14: Validation of Research Statements

Index	Statements	Confirmation Methods
S1	Luxury goods emit a status signal.	» Descriptive analysis » Reliability analysis » Regression analysis
S2	Added luxury value ALV is stronger for a luxury good than for a non-luxury.	» Descriptive analysis » Reliability analysis » Regression analysis
S3	The luxury signal can be moderated.	» Descriptive analysis » Reliability analysis
S4	A relationship exists between luxury and each of the ALV sub-constructs.	» Correlation analysis » Regression analysis
S5	A structural relationship exists between input and output items of the luxury model.	» Correlation analysis » Regression analysis

S6	Despite low affinity towards luxury, added luxury value may be perceived in case of a strong and clear original signal.	» Regression analysis
S7	Our results are structurally consistent and coherent across countries.	» Cross cultural study, descriptive analysis
S8	Our results are consistent and coherent independent of the maturity of a country in relation to luxury consumption.	» Cross cultural study, descriptive analysis

The results also led to a revision of the model using factor analysis. The revision does not change the model substantially. The fundamental relationships remain unchanged including input, output and moderating elements.

- We exchange the original set of input sub-constructs ("antecedents") with the set extracted utilizing factor analysis. Rationale is that the new set sharpens the dimensions and adds emotional facets to the antecedents. It also includes formerly hidden aspects like "VIP treatment" and "privacy at point of sale".
- We keep the original output set as factor analysis did not add too much additional insights to the added luxury value components. The exception is the sub-construct "celebrity-alike", which we add to the set of added luxury value components.

The luxury framework and model have proven robust in their ability to explain luxury. The model is a powerful tool to measure input-output relationships and distill managerial strategies.

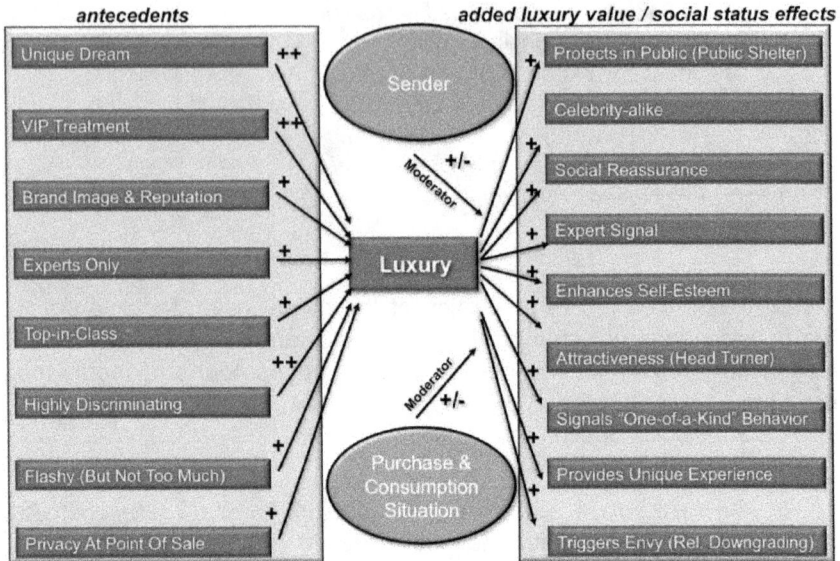

Figure 23: Model of Luxury – Revised

Attitude Based Luxury Definition

The confirmation of the luxury model leads to an additional definition of luxury, which is based on attitudes and considerations. Compared to our original core definition of luxury framed in Chapter 5, the attitude based core definition emphasizes emotional facets – i.e. aspect of a dream – of luxury as well as psychological consideration and expectations.

> **Luxury is a unique dream and it is driven by brand image and reputation. It requires a high degree of expertise – in making and consuming. It is top-in-class, highly discriminating and flashy (but not too much). It requires a VIP treatment and privacy at the point of sale.**

Both definitions describe luxuries, but with different precision. While the original definition emphasizes added luxury value – i.e. unique experience in combination with a perceived enhancement or reinforcement of the social position – the attitude-based definition accentuates the antecedents of luxury that lead to luxury perception. It also includes the aspect of brand equity.

The key implication for luxury managers is the requirement to steer the dream perception by managing luxury brands in an appropriate way. Also the other antecedents of luxury need to be managed in order to create perceivable added luxury value.

Chapter 16: Perceptions and Geographical Differences

Objective:
Assessment how people perceive luxuries

Key aspects:
- Results of luxury study are presented
- Personality trait perception seems to evolve positively
- Significant enhancement of almost all social status dimensions
- People seem to have sensitive "antenna" for luxury signal
- Significant moderation effect observed (e.g. fakes)
- Rationale for tendency toward discreet luxury identified
- Results appear consistent across geographies

Perceptions

Model and study results obtained in Europe (Germany and France) indicate that a luxury good has the power to enhance the perception of a person related to that particular item.

As an example of the study, a woman was perceived more positive when she was wearing a luxury dress. Particularly, personality traits that were evaluated somewhat medium when the person did wear a "normal" dress (H&M), suddenly evolved towards a perceived personal strength once dressed in "luxury" (Chanel). In an other example, in which a woman was driving either a rather normal car (Volkswagen) or a luxury car (Bentley), a significant enhancement of almost all social status – hence added luxury value – dimensions of our model could be observed (Figure 24). In short, people seem to be perceived in a more positive way once surrounded with luxury.

The research further reveals that people seem to have a very sensitive "antenna" for the luxury signal and its clarity, strength, and consistency.

The moderating variables of the model were tested by introducing additional information on evaluated people.

In one example, a man was observed and evaluated while he was wearing a Patek Philippe luxury watch. After study participants evaluated the added luxury value dimensions, they were given the information that the watch was a fake. In a re-evaluation, the perception of the men dropped significantly over most dimensions (Figure 25).

In contrast, adding more luxury goods, for example connecting the woman in the Chanel dress with a private plane and other luxury items and thus making the situation perceived as more consistent, produced results of very strong perceived added luxury value.

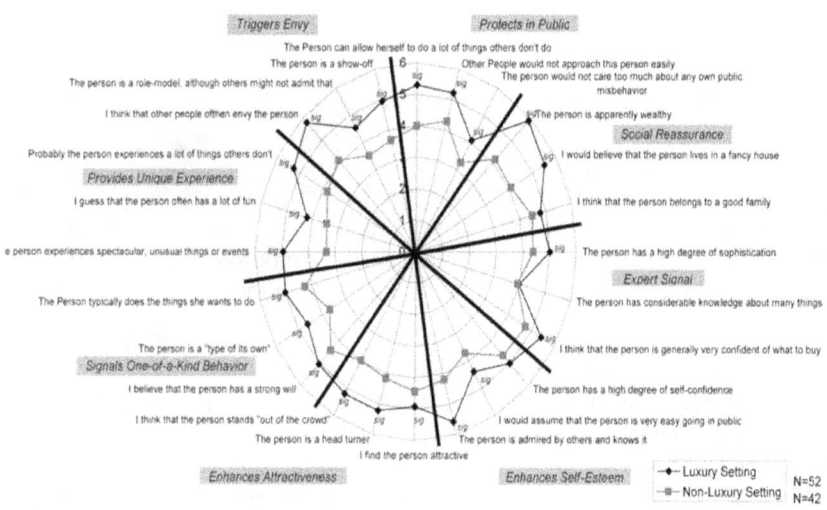

Figure 24: Perception of a woman in luxury

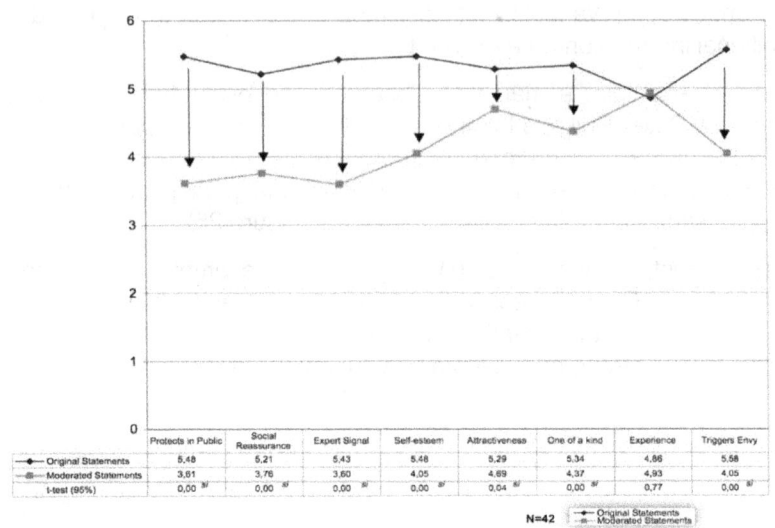

	Protects in Public	Social Reassurance	Expert Signal	Self-esteem	Attractiveness	One of a kind	Experience	Triggers Envy
Original Statements	5,48	5,21	5,43	5,48	5,29	5,34	4,86	5,58
Moderated Statements	3,61	3,76	3,60	4,05	4,89	4,37	4,93	4,05
t-test (95%)	0,00 s/	0,00 s/	0,00 s/	0,00 s/	0,04 s/	0,00 s/	0,77	0,00 s/

N=42

Figure 25: Effect of Moderation (Fake watch)

As a result, any deviation from an individually pre-defined norm may lead to strong changes in the interpretation of the luxury signal. The re-interpretation may affect several of the luxury output indicators at the same time and may strongly decrease or enhance the evaluation of people.

This seems to confirm the rationale for the tendency towards discreet or stealth luxury with increased luxury consumption intensity: If people show off too much or behave in a socially inappropriate way, they may not achieve the intended social status effects. Even worse, they may decrease the status perception strongly. On the other hand, a carefully chosen and very consistent individual luxury consumption strategy may lead to very strong positive luxury signal amplification.

144

Geographical Differences?

Can those findings be applied across countries and cultures or are they limited to distinct geographical areas? There is no indication from theory about any constraint of applying the luxury model universally across countries and cultures. On the contrary, when we dissected the set of luxury drivers as fundamental part of the model we utilized many observations, examples and findings from America, Europe and Asia.

However, as a check for negatives, an additional cross-cultural study with a small sample size was conducted in USA, Japan and China to produce further evidence for universal application. The sample sizes were below the threshold of 30, which is the minimum sample to assume any given distribution becoming close to normal distribution. As normal distribution is a precondition for most statistical tests, only tendencies were assessed.

We evaluated spider plots of mean scores comparing luxury and non-luxury situations and also plots of mean scores comparing original with moderated situations. Central assumption: If luxury has universal power, then added luxury value should be perceived across countries and cultures in a comparable way.

Germany, France, USA, Japan and China have different "maturities" on a level of market evolution in regard to luxury consumption. While we would classify Germany, France, USA and Japan as rather "mature", with a relatively high GDP per capita and a high density of luxury brands and stores, China is – overall – still a relatively inexperienced society in regards to luxury consumption due to historical developments. However, observing development and availability of luxury brands, China is catching up fast, especially in mega cities like Shanghai or Beijing.

Despite differences in culture, luxury "maturity" and possibly brand perceptions, the results seem to be consistent. The check for negatives did not indicate any constraint in the use of the luxury model across countries. The luxury contexts produced considerable added luxury value in the study, and moderating variables were able to influence the luxury signal in all countries in a similar way.

As a result, there is strong indication, both from theory and from the cross cultural study, that the model may work universally and that added luxury value is perceived in a similar way across cultures and geographies. What may differ are the goods that are perceived as luxuries, dependent on the available brands, the brand image and the standards within a country or community.

Note on Generalization of Results

The results of the study were produced by testing individual situations. We have chosen a test design to be able to measure luxury in a relatively unbiased way. However, the methodology does not provide an absolute proof that the results are generalizable for all possible situations. Indeed we could show that some sub-constructs may be significantly linked to luxury in one situation, while they may not be a significant added luxury value component in another situation. Although we cannot detail the ability of luxury to provide added luxury value for all theoretically possible situations, theory and produced results do not provide any indication for the opposite. In many situations one or more added luxury value dimensions can be expected to be enhanced by luxury goods. The complete study design and results can be reviewed in Langer (2008).

Chapter 17: Branding Strategies for the Luxury Manager

Objective:
Provide key strategies for the profitable management of luxury

Key aspects:
- 6 "L" of Luxury – six winning strategies to manage luxury brands
- Long-term perspective - importance of competitive advantage
- Dreams and desires shift – constant adaptation needed
- Unique Luxury Proposition
- Luxury pricing
- Profit relationships for luxuries
- Luxury portfolio management
- Luxury Life Cycle – avoid the luxury unit trap

Key Strategies for the Profitable Management of Luxury

As Ohmae (1982, p.12) points out, "Analysis is the critical starting point of strategic thinking… In strategic thinking, one first seeks a clear understanding of the particular character of each element of a situation and then makes the fullest possible use of human brainpower to restructure the elements in the most advantageous way."

In other words, strategy starts with assessing the situation, capabilities, abilities to win, competition and consumers, which can be done utilizing the tool of the luxury category assessment. Out of this assessment, a long-term plan of actions needs to be derived, with the objective to achieve a sustainable competitive advantage.

Given our findings, a strategy of sustainable competitive advantage means being able to continuously create a higher ratio of perceived

$$\frac{\text{Added Luxury Value}}{\text{Luxury Premium}}$$

by consumers in comparison to competing offers (see also Figure 20, luxury's strategic triangle).

In a context of dreams and desires in which luxuries fulfill needs of people, it may not be easy to defend and maintain a strategic advantage on the long run, as dreams and desires can be moving targets, prone to change. Nevertheless, we suggest that it is of utmost importance to distill clear plans of what to do and what not to do in order to succeed and make profit in the luxury segment.

The starting points for strategies will be very different depending on industry, category or competition. Therefore, strategies that we propose in the following can never be complete in an absolute way.

However, our aim is to distill key strategies, which we suggest as "best practice" and "most appropriate" in a general luxury context. Those strategies will be detailed and substantiated with suggested sub-strategies and examples.

We identified six key strategies for managers, which we call the six "L" of luxury. They are visualized in Figure 26 and summarized in Table 15 with parameters and rationale.

The strategy "Link-to-Consumer" includes the maximization of individualization, hence creating a "one of a kind" product in the most extreme case. The strategy "Leverage Pricing" describes the exploitation of the up-pricing potential of a luxury good. In other words, it tackles the question "how high is high" in relation to luxuries in order to maximize profitability from a pricing perspective.

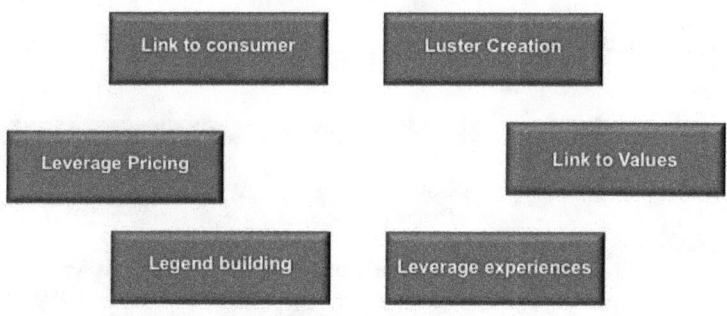

Figure 26: Six "L" of Luxury – Key Strategies for Managers

We identified "Legend-Building" as important for luxuries, thus it is consequently one of the key strategies for the profitable management of luxury. The strategy of "Luster-Creation" refers to selling objects that may be perceived as or that may even become a "piece of art".

One of our proposed key strategies is "Link-to-Values", in relation to being consistent with social values as well as being consistent with the DNA of a luxury brand. Similarly, the strategy "Leverage Experiences" is an important strategy in order to keep a luxury desired on a high level. It includes the management of surprise.

The strategies incorporate lessons from luxury drivers, luxury pricing and luxury model. In our eyes they provide a solid managerial framework for steering luxury in a profitable and sustainable way.

Table 15: Six "L" of Luxury – Key Strategies for Managers

Strategy and Guiding Question	Selected Parameters	Rationale
Link-to-Consumer: Maximize individualization. How exclusive can you be?	» One of a kind. » Limitation. » Refined service. » Privacy and security. » Lifespan relationship. » Exclusive membership.	» Strategy of top tier of "most luxurious" categories. » Key aspect of luxury driver analysis. » Key aspect of luxury model.
Leverage Pricing: Exploit up-pricing potential. How high is high?	» Price sensitivity. » Willingness-to-pay. » Investment. » Reduce social pressure.	» Strategy of top tier of "most luxurious" categories. » Key aspect of luxury model.
Legend-Building: Create the most unique image. How legendary can you be?	» Image and Awareness. » Premiums of consumption. » Superiority. » Values.	» Strategy of top tier of "most luxurious" categories. » Key aspect of luxury driver analysis.
Luster-Creation: Sell a "piece-of-art". How special can you be?	» Focus on every detail. » Deliver highest quality. » Cost management.	» Strategy of top tier of "most luxurious" categories. » Key aspect of luxury driver analysis.
Link-to-Values: Be consistent with social values and with the brand DNA. How consistent can you be?	» Luxury reliability. » Luxury validity. » Social compatibility. » Consistent price positioning. » Consistent portfolio.	» Key aspect of luxury model. » Criteria for sustainable. competitive advantage. » Key aspect of luxury driver analysis.
Leverage Experiences: Manage surprise. How interesting can you be?	» Not-done-yet. » Create dreams. » Ultimate experience. » Manage surprise.	» Strategy of top tier of "most luxurious" categories. » Key aspect of luxury driver analysis.

Link-to-Consumer: Maximize Individualization

How exclusive can you be? We have shown that there is a clear correlation of exclusivity, scarcity, individualization and perception of luxury. The more individualized and exclusive an item becomes, the more it creates added luxury value: Closely inspecting the most luxurious goods of our category assessment, all were very rare, in the extreme available only once. In case of lingerie, the limitation to one single item helped to create a total value, which is five million times higher than the "base" product.

This leads to a provoking thought: if someone would own all five cars of the Bugatti Veyron Pur Sang edition, the potential destruction of four cars could possibly increase the value of the remaining car far above the combined value of the original five. This was indicated in the assessment of the car category applying the luxury index: we concluded that there seems to be a potential for a significantly more expensive top-tier.

In the game of luxury, being able to create a "one-of-a-kind" product or service, completely individualized, somewhat private, possibly discrete and eventually with high security standards, is a very important strategy for profitable, sustainable competitive advantage or even dominance. We call this point of differentiation ULP, the unique luxury proposition, and visualize its key facets in Figure 27.

An important aspect of ULP is price as one of its parameters. A high price point makes the total offer unique and helps to raise expectation and experience. Thus a high absolute price with a high luxury index has to be integral part of the unique luxury proposition. A finding at the California Institute of Technology underlines this. Researchers at the institute could show that the enjoyment of wine is heightened if a person is told that it is an expensive one (Westcott 2008).

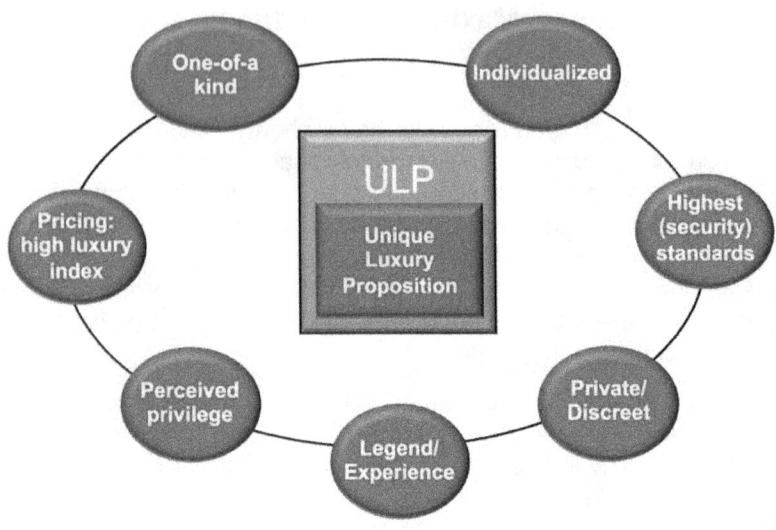

Figure 27: Unique Luxury Proposition ULP

A brand that is able to offer a completely individualized product also has a high likelihood to establish a lifespan relationship with consumers. Good examples are shoemakers for hand made shoes, a tailor for made-to-measure suits or a couturier in haute couture. If you have your measures at one shoemaker, the likelihood that you will commission shoes again and again is rather high, due to individualization and convenience. Thus the "one-of-a-kind" strategy also shields off competition, decreases price sensitivity and stimulates loyalty.

This can be further enhanced through some of the hurdles that have been discussed in the luxury driver analysis, like the need to qualify for a purchase. If not everyone can be a client of a certain brand, the willingness to lose that privilege is expected to be low.

Leverage Pricing: Exploit Up-Pricing Potential

How high is high? The answer to this question is the key task for any manager of luxury goods as this is the direct driver of profitability. As luxury goods create added luxury value that may be hundred, thousand or even million times higher than the functional value of its category, assessing the willingness-to-pay – which reflects the perceived total value of the product including the added luxury value – is decisive. Figure 28 visualizes the three possible pricing scenarios:

–   Scenario 1 shows an underpriced luxury good. Consequence is insufficient profitability, as the profit potential of the luxury product is not exploited. Furthermore, an underpriced luxury good risks not to be perceived as luxury in a clear way. If something is overly available to the masses, it lacks exclusivity. As Prabhakar (2007b) states in the opening quote of this chapter, the most expensive product signals that the owner can afford the one and only top product. Underpriced luxury risks losing this status and might not deliver sufficient profitability, thus the strategy is not sustainable.

–   Scenario 2 visualizes a product that is priced "just right", as price reflects total value including added luxury value. The profit potential is fully exploited, and price positioning is consistent with consumer perceptions. This strategy is sustainable if the cost of producing the luxury product is controlled and market parameters do not change.

–   Scenario 3 has the consequence that the product will most likely not sell, as added luxury value is too small to match the total perceived value of the product to the price. Although we expect lower price sensitivity for luxury compared other categories, exceeding the total value with the price is unlikely to be sustainable in the long run.

However, the willingness-to-pay is increasingly difficult to measure the more exclusive a product becomes, especially if it is built-to-order and only exists once. Conjoint measurement techniques require a sophisticated test set-up, which would be difficult – if not impossible – to apply with individual luxury consumers. Therefore, for exclusive luxury goods the willingness-to-pay needs to be explored by qualitative means.

For example by trying to understand the target group in-depth and gradually exploring the maximum price points.

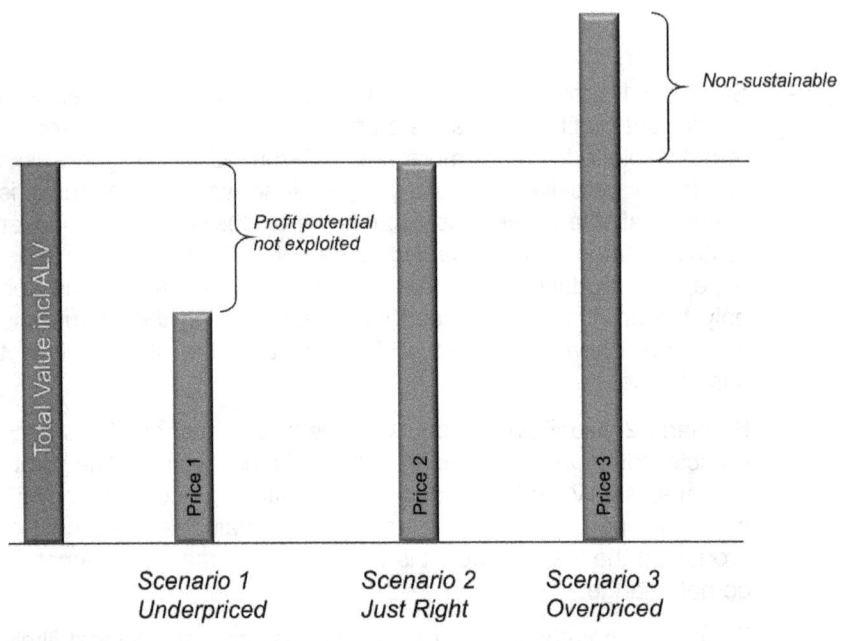

Figure 28: Luxury Pricing Scenarios

A limitation is that managers of top-tier products usually cannot afford the products they are selling and do not live the lives of their clientele. However, gaining insights about the target group is key. A marketing manager for a luxury fashion brand needs to understand the dynamics of the business of the clients. Not living the lives of the target group puts a significant risk to failing in terms of understanding the emotional drivers of the customers and of setting the price right.

Strategies to gain information about the willingness-to-pay and the price sensitivity of the target group in order to set the pricing right could be:

154

- Cooperating with target group members as consultants.

- Installing a target group "investigation force". A small group of people close to the target group who have the task to actively interact with target group members at events, private views, or other occasions.

- Attracting "brand ambassadors", people who are familiar with the target group and accepted within. Similar to the investigation force, their task is to interact, identify insights and influence the target group.

- Exploit personal contacts of the top managers of the luxury brand as they themselves are attractive counterparts for luxury customers. Those contacts allow a direct interaction with the target group and may also help to enhance willingness-to-pay.

- Close monitoring of the market e.g. on fairs, via desk research and internet screening. Companies who serve the top-tier need to know what is going on and especially if new, more expensive products with a new unique luxury propositions ULP have been launched.

- Launch an overly expensive "decoy" product in order to test the willingness-to-pay. What does it mean? We understand a "decoy" product as a product mainly intended to test a brand's price potential. It should be overly expensive, even compared to the rest of the brand's portfolio, and mark the top end of the range in terms of craftsmanship and performance. Incorporating the lessons on difficulty to sell the decoy, information about the willingness-to-pay can be generated. If the product is overly expensive and the cost of making has been carefully investigated, a pricing decoy can be launched at limited risk, especially if it is built-to-order upon consumer request. Additionally, such a decoy can serve to boost the image of the luxury brand by setting it apart from others.

- Sponsoring events that are regarded as vital to the key buyers. This offers the opportunity to speak with the target group outside of the usual context and explore wishes, dreams and thoughts, leading to insights about pricing.

To set the pricing for a top-tier product, the parameters that we utilized for the luxury category analysis can serve as further indicators, especially to indicate a too low price benchmarked with other categories. Both, luxury index and median analysis help to indicate if the relative price points fits comparably. Nevertheless it is also decisive to assess, whether the product is designed in such a unique way, that the price point is reflected by added luxury value.

Also the moment of sale is important in pricing a luxury good. If the sale would be done in a rather rational place, like the conference room in the office of the potential buyer, rational considerations might decrease the willingness-to-pay.

Instead, if the sale is done at a dinner in a fancy restaurant, at a racetrack after experiencing the acceleration of a sports car or at marina after spending a day on a yacht, a more emotional mood can help to decrease price-sensitivity and thus increase the willingness-to-pay.

Legend-Building: Create the Most Unique Image

How legendary can you be? A luxury brand should clearly be a legend or it should have one, as all top-tier items of our category assessment have a story to tell.

A legend increases the individual positioning of a luxury product or brand. Our category analysis clearly shows that practically all top-tier offers in luxury feature such a legend. There are several strategies:

- A legend of craftsmanship: Starting from years of preparation to acquire the necessary skills to craft a product. Those may be followed by years and unbelievable efforts of building the good. Part of the legend should be attention to every detail and the ability to deliver an individualized product. Bottom line: The combined efforts make the product truly unique and difficult to copy.

- A legend of beauty and glitz, involving the world's most admired people – film stars and models at "once in a lifetime" moments – like the Oscar night. Bottom line: The exclusive setting makes the product truly unique and adds glamour, visibility and attraction to the brand.

- A legend of provocation, danger and sex may work for some luxury brands, like for Gucci during the Tom Ford era, creating the image of breaking out of everyday routines. Benefits and limitations were discussed in Chapter 10.

- A legend of seriousness and values.

A legend built around the efforts required to master the consumption of the product – the premiums of consumption: A sports car that requires a private racetrack access to be fully utilized. An haute couture dress that requires a strict diet. A yacht that requires a mooring in a marina, a crew and eventually a license to pilot the boat. Bottom line: as it is difficult to command the product, the product becomes more exclusive and less accessible.

- A legend of individuality – in terms of creating a cult around the founders' mission or in terms of dramatizing that each consumer can underline his or her individuality with one of the brand's items.

- A legend built around the heritage of the brand – in terms of aviation history, travel history, yachting history, sports history, culture and art history etc. Bottom line: the linkage to the brand to history makes it more special and unique, difficult to copy.

- A legend built around "having the future now". Especially for a brand that is entering new grounds and that does not have a history, a legend around mastering the future can be an interesting differentiator.

- A legend of superiority. As luxury is connected to best-in-class performance on specific items, creating a legend of superiority may be a powerful strategy. Focusing on functional superiority, a superior experience or highlighting the superior price may execute the strategy.

- A legend of eco-friendliness, respecting nature, animals and wildlife by minimizing the ecological footprints.

In terms of competitive strategy it is important that the story is unique, involving and relevant to the target group. Given the high importance of luxury products for consumers, the story also needs to be authentic in order to be credible and sustainable.

Furthermore, it is important to create awareness for the story or legend: For example, there are cases when a construction project including several expensive houses manages to have a celebrity officially moving in first (for free or at discounted rates). Once the legend spreads, many others may be interested in also acquiring a house with the intention to live in a "celebrity neighborhood".

As we pointed out, it is essential to manage the image permanently. This requires skills to keep the legend alive by fueling the brand with performance and news and by making sure that the brand always remains part of the target group's "dream". This is a very individual task, depending on the specifics of each brand. However, past examples on luxury brands that lost luster and appeal are clear warning signs that a luxury brand can never rely on past performance only if it wants to avoid becoming irrelevant.

Luster-Creation: Sell a Piece of Art

How special can you be? Luxury is – in a sense – all about creating something truly special and offering a means of differentiation. Art offers such a differentiation as a piece of art usually comes at just one item. Our luxury category assessment showed that practically all top-tier products moved far away from a basic functional product towards a piece of art, decorated with diamonds, specially crafted, truly exclusive.

This formula is a key strategy for luxury: to make the product special enough to be perceived as a piece of art, e.g. by collaborating with artists and top craftsmen. We discussed examples and executions in the luxury driver analysis.

While being highly attractive in terms of creating added luxury value by a specific ULP, the strategy requires very precise financial planning and a thorough business plan reflecting capital cost, labor cost and material cost. This also implies an enormous amount of research and development efforts and expenditures. Just imagine the expenditures to develop and test the 1001 horsepower engine of the Bugatti Veyron including the production of prototypes. Those investments need to be re-financed via a very limited number of cars only.

In sum, the "piece of art" strategy requires a huge amount of creativity and craftsmanship skills, resulting in comparably high cost of goods for production. Also, very limited production numbers lead to an enormous production complexity and typically high cash net working capital requirements. As the Economist (2007) highlights, luxury is capital intensive.

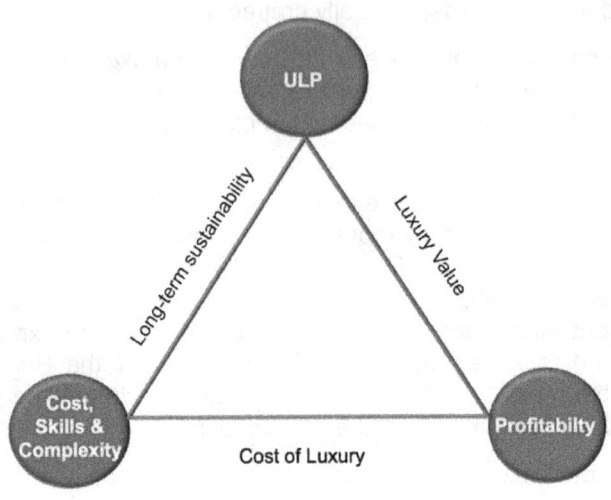

Figure 29: Profit Relationship for Luxuries

We provide a visualization of the profit relationship for luxuries in Figure 29: ULP and cost, skills and complexity need to be managed in a profitable way to achieve long-term sustainability. Hence, luxury value has to exceed the cost of providing the luxury.

This underlines the strong managerial interrelation between luxury price management and luxury cost management as a critical success factor in the management of luxury goods. In a sense, the pricing strategy determines how much a product can become a piece of art. On the other hand, once the product becomes art, one can charge high relative and absolute prices.

An important facet of the strategy is to stimulate the desire for collecting by selling additional items to existing consumers, similar to collecting art. To execute this strategy, it is important to create close relationships with the consumers, deeply understand their insights and offer a relevant portfolio of collectibles. Apart from strategies discussed on relationship building, gaining insights and influencing consumers, exclusive mega events can do the job.

160

Link-to-Values: Be Consistent with Social Values and the Brand DNA

How consistent can you be in terms of social values and brand DNA? Given our findings, consistency with both is a key strategy for the long-term profitable management of luxury.

Social Values

Let's start with social values: Of course a brand can and sometimes needs to be provoking, like in the case of Gucci. Nevertheless we have shown that ignoring social key trends can have negative influence on the luxury perception. Given the high involvement and symbolic relationships with luxury goods, we suggest that consumers expect much higher standards for luxury products in terms of social values compared to average products.

If a luxury brand claims to be environmental-friendly, the promise will most likely be closely tracked and observed by consumers and may lead to strong negative reactions in case of non-compliance. Thus, authenticity is of utmost importance. Strategies to ensure the compliance are:

- Installation of a code of conduct with sanctions in case of non-compliance.
- Clear rules, encouraging product developers to spend resources on ensuring the compliance of the brand with social values. Lexus, as an example, already offers most lines with hybrid technology and is therefore able to position itself as the "greener choice" versus other luxury car brands. If consumer expectations towards fuel efficiency further accelerate, this can be a tremendous competitive advantage and source of ULP.

- Openly and pro-actively communicate on social efforts and achievements.

Brand DNA

Equally, the DNA of the brand needs to be reflected in every detail of a luxury brand's touch points with consumers, from communication on the phone, e-mails and mails, brochures, fairs, products, materials and dedication to even the smallest detail. Managerial strategies include:

- Clear top-management dedication and commitment to establishing a corporate culture of highest aspiration in terms of quality and building up the brand image.

- Clear vision and principles, communicated within the company and sanctioned if not followed.

- Consistency in price positioning of a luxury brand across product lines and categories. If a brand is positioned in the top-tier of a category, this positioning should be consequently executed. We have discussed the danger of entry point offers that are inconsistent with the brand DNA. As a luxury brand is not competing on lowest price, but on creating added luxury value, all items have to help to underline the brand perception by consumers. Rather than offering cheaper entry point items that compromise on quality and brand values, luxury brands should rather offer financing, leasing or fractional ownership schemes for consumers, for whom the brand might be financially out of reach.

- Establish and develop excellent press contacts and refined public relation techniques. This allows influencing the way the brand is presented in media, also in terms of product reviews and performance tests.

Consistency and Precision of Portfolio Management

Figure 30 visualizes the growth trap for luxury brands in a life cycle model: In Phase I a luxury brand is extremely focused with a highly exclusive offer, low number of units and high profitability per unit. In Phase II the brand offers congruent line extensions, increasing the number of units and typically decreasing the profitability per unit slightly due to higher complexity. Phase III describes incongruent line extensions, leading to a strong increase in units and further loss of profitability per unit. If a luxury brand does not take countermeasures in this phase, it risks the loss of perceived luxuriousness (Phase IV). In this phase the most profitable customers leave the brand and seek more exclusive brands. Due to a decrease of sales of the top-end-products the profitability per unit strongly decreases. In addition, as the brand loses its appeal, also mid-tier consumers typically leave, leading to a negative spiral of combined decrease of units and profitability.

How broad can a luxury brand become? We suggest that as long as the luxury signal is managed in a very clear way and as long as exclusivity is maintained through pricing or other access hurdles, luxury brands can become broader. The challenge is to balance broadness, craftsmanship and a very distinct and unique performance and experience in a very consistent way. It is also important to always take the fit to the brand DNA into account and to create a clear unique luxury proposition ULP. Managing exclusivity and high sales numbers at the same time is extremely delicate. The top tier luxury customers can afford literally anything and will not buy the same brand everybody else has or a brand that is inconsistent in terms of positioning.

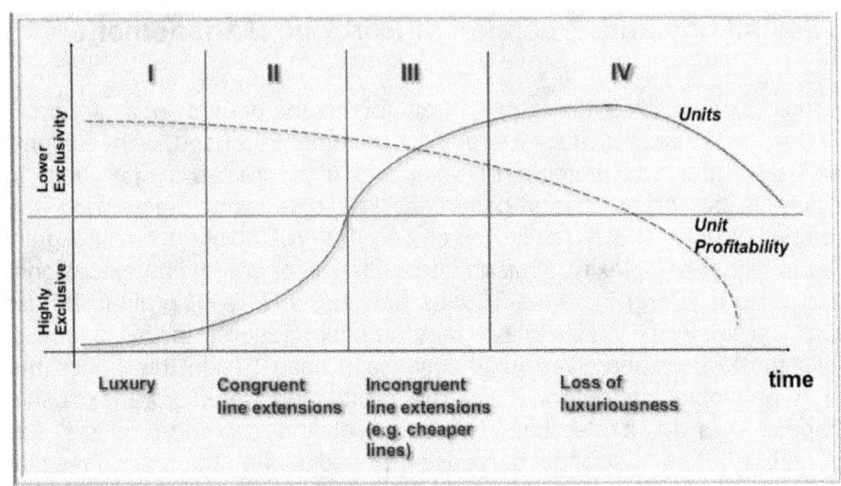

Figure 30: Luxury Life Cycle: Unit Growth Trap

We suggest that even small deficits in managing the fit of the experience, heritage and quality, may have strong negative effects on the luxury brand equity.

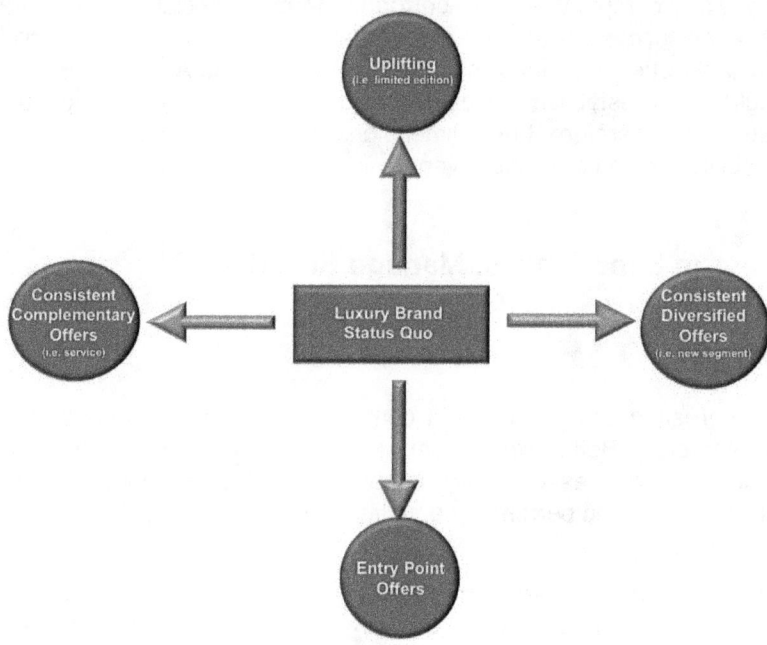

Figure 31: Luxury Strategies for Portfolio Management

Figure 31 indicates portfolio strategies for luxury brands distilled from above analysis: Uplifting, hence the value-creating offers with higher price points, is a proven strategy for luxury watch brands and top-end car brands with significantly up-priced limited editions. Offering diversified but consistently positioned goods is a strategy ensures consistency of positioning. Consistent complementary offers can be services like driver training on a racetrack for sports cars. Entry point offers are common practice for luxury brands; however, they also imply highest risk for the clarity of the luxury signal.

Challenger brands that may aspire to be perceived as luxury brands need to closely follow those strategies and be very cautious to manage the luxury signals carefully. As challenger brands still do not have a clear and strong luxury signal, any mistake in brand building is likely to strongly set back the intended luxury perception.

If a luxury company failed to perform in terms of social values or brand DNA even occasionally, we doubt that it would be able to build a sustainable business platform in the luxury segment. At least it would be difficult to re-establish credibility and brand equity among luxury consumers. Therefore both dimensions are directly related to brand profitability both on cost and revenue side.

Leverage Experiences: Manage Surprise

How interesting can you be? If it comes to luxury, you should better be very interesting. Both, luxury driver analysis and luxury category analysis indicated surprise as one very important facet about luxury. Surprise through unexpected performance, ultimate and not-done-yet experiences, and fulfilling dreams.

Therefore the management of surprise is a key strategy in luxury marketing. What feels like a surprise for the consumers needs to be carefully prepared and orchestrated by the luxury company. Strategies include:

- Analysis and deep understanding of competition. If a luxury brand tries to surprise on a dimension that other brands manage much better, it will fail in the market place.

- Analysis and deep understanding of the consumers in terms of their experiences, expertise and expectations. A luxury sports car brand that intends to surprise a sheik in terms of performance should clarify before, whether the sheik owns a private racetrack and several Ferraris or Lamborghinis and is – thus – already an expert for the category. Such a person would be difficult to be surprised on the performance dimension. A surprise element could be instead to sell him a trip to a Formula 1 event, where he can meet the stars backstage and maybe even drive one of the original racecars under guidance of a Formula 1 pro.

- Define a clear "passport" or rulebook for the ULP that indicates on which dimensions the brand has to deliver superior experiences. Set up key performance indicators (KPI) how to measure the brand's performance on the defined ULP set.

- As the repetition of a surprise is normally not surprising anymore, it is key to install a managed creative process, in which new surprising ideas and new ultimate experienced are constantly developed. This also includes an integration of the "surprise management" and "dream maintenance" into the company culture, promotion and reward systems. A company that is able to excel in this dimension can very likely install a sustainable competitive advantage.

- Dare to offer unusual or incongruent services and products, as long as they fit to the brand DNA.

It is evident that the management of surprise also has measurable implications on revenue and cost side, thus it has direct influence on the profitability. The more experienced the luxury consumers are, the more difficult the task becomes.

On the other hand, surprising the world's richest can turn out an extremely profitable strategy due to their ability to compensate the added value created by paying overly expensive prices: When the world's richest call to buy a unique experience, a luxury manager should be able to find a way to be the person on the other end of the line.

Chapter 18: Concluding Remarks and Pitfalls

So what is luxury all about? When we started, it seemed clear that luxury has got to be expensive, exclusive, scarce and special, a dream making life more beautiful: A special experience and a sensual pleasure, able to differentiate, while often requiring some effort in acquisition and consumption.

All those points have been confirmed throughout the book. On top we were able to reveal luxury's hidden aspects: luxury is a "tool" to turn heads and become more attractive, a shelter and protector in public, a "tool" to signal expertise, a source of improved self-esteem and self-perception, a "tool" that enables a mindset-change towards new experiences. And it is something that makes people feel like celebrities.

Those aspects have been identified as key output variables of luxury consumption. They are the conscious or even unconscious rationale why people buy luxuries: Luxuries help to define the individual position within the social context and they are both: a group marker and a separator.

If people invest significant sums on luxury goods during their lifespan, the top-tier of products has to be of significant importance. The concept of added luxury value ALV as a result of the luxury signal processing enables one to explain this high individual importance.

In short: with this book we decode luxury in an unprecedented, comprehensive and detailed way, processing the state-of-the art of the research on luxury and related topics. As stated initially, this book covers the key content of the authors' book "Luxury: Marketing & Management" in an essential, more compact format. To those who want to take the knowledge about luxury to the next level and get additional inspiration by more background and more examples, the original textbook would seem to be a natural next step to read.

Our findings allow both, researchers and managers to have a deeper understanding of luxury, its facets and aspects. We confirmed that – similar to a picture where red is always red independent from the likes of the picture – luxury follows distinct rules and codes. It has certain properties and effects, to a large extent independent of the likes or dislikes or people towards luxury. We showed that luxury goods are important in the lives of most people as they help to satisfy needs.

Managers are provided with definitions, core aspects, a broad set of luxury drivers, structural relationships between input and output items, and aspects of luxury pricing. Among other aspects, luxury goods seem to be more stable to recession: people have lower price sensitivity and a higher willingness-to-pay. Loyalty is usually higher compared to non-luxuries.

The management of luxury requires a very specific marketing approach, significantly different from mass-market goods. However, there are indications that not all of today's luxury brands execute a "luxury approach" in an appropriate way. This becomes especially evident by assessing the portfolio management of selected luxury brands and by understanding the luxury life cycle.

We show that all categories have the potential to develop a luxury tier. To do so, we propose an easy-to-apply way to assess and benchmark categories, with the luxury index as new and straightforward manager tool. An outcome of our benchmarking is that the luxury index differs strongly across categories, which shows that there is a huge potential for luxury goods still to be exploited.

How to capitalize on this unused potential? We frame six key strategies to manage luxury (six "L" of luxury) including the unique luxury proposition ULP. We also highlight possible implications of strategies on profitability. Finally, we highlight potential risks, limitations and pitfalls.

In sum, we offer a comprehensive and convenient toolbox for managers to be able to produce better and more sustainable results in managing luxury.

Researchers are provided with a comprehensive framework of luxury which significantly broadens the research status quo, and which includes definition, a structural model, and a set of items and sub-constructs of luxury. The model is validated in a quantitative cross-cultural study.

We have revealed that luxury is an extremely complex and fascinating topic, where sustainable success in the market place depends on deep understanding and the choice of the right strategies. We have shown that luxury goods may be beautiful and add beauty to a person; they state "I am unique" and they might even add a glimpse of eternity due to their extraordinary qualities. They are inspiring and alluring. They represent a unique dream.

Luxury is always on the move. Today's luxury is able to attract consumers around the globe. Then people buy it and – if not managed properly – it may become too common. Eventually, it is not perceived as luxury anymore. In the meantime, the top-tier of customers has already headed to the next object of desire that guarantees exclusivity and status. Just to be followed by others, soon.

To underline the appeal of luxury, we conclude with a quote of Vorasarun (2007, online) asking the rhetorical question, "Who wants to party like a rock star, when you can party like a billionaire?" In short, this is what luxury and the desire for it is all about.

References

20ltd.com (2012), Company Homage. www.20ltd.com, Aug 15, 2012

Alba, Joseph W. and J. Wesley Hutchinson (1987), "Dimensions of Consumer Expertise", *Journal of Consumer Research*, 13:4, 411–454

Alderman, Liz (Nov 29, 2007), "In Russian luxury market, companies strategize to reach the rich consumer", *International Herald Tribune*, Internet edition

Aloisson (2007), Company Homepage, www.aloisson.com, Oct 28, 2007

Atlanta dBusinessNews (Apr 15, 2007), "Porsche Named Top Prestigious Luxury Automobile Brand for 2007", Internet edition

Arain, Fauzia (Jan 3, 2008), "Living the lux life", *Chicago Tribune*, Internet edition

Autobild (2005), "Jaguar X-Type: Nur ein feinerer Mondeo?", 29/2005, Aug 8, 2005, Internet edition

Autobild (2012), "Radikal-Roadster mit 700 PS", Mar 5, 2012, Internet edition

Autoblog.com (2007), "Dyno Dino: Baby Ferrari test mule spotted", Jul 11, 2007, Internet edition

Babej, Marc E. and Tim Pollak (2006), "Making 'Exclusive' Exclusive Again", *Forbes,* Aug 9, 2006, Internet edition

Bass, Shermakaye (Sep 17, 2007), "Luxury as world increases its star power", *International Herald Tribune*, Internet edition

Basu, Amiya, Tridib Mazumdar and S. P. Raj (2003), "Indirect Network Externality Effects on Product Attributes", *Marketing Science* 22, 209–221

BBC (2010), "India's Ambani hosts party for 'world's priciest home'", Nov 27, 2010, Internet edition

BBC (2012), "China luxury sales 'driven by the ultra rich'", Jun 6, 2012, Internet edition

Belk, Russell W. (1985), "Materialism: Trait Aspects of Living in the Material World", *Journal of Consumer Research* 12:3, 265–280

Belk, Russell W. (1988), "Possessions and the Extended Self", *Journal of Consumer Research,* 15:2 139–168

Belk, Russell W., Gueliz Ger and Soren Askegaard (2003), "The Fire of Desire: A Multisited Inquiry into Consumer Passion", *Journal of Consumer Research* 30, 326–351

Bentley (2007), Company Homepage, www.bentleymotors.com, Sep 22, 2007

Bentley (2012), Company Homepage, www.bentleymotors.com, Aug 24, 2012

Beverland, Michael B. (2004), "An Exploration of the Luxury Wine Trade", *International Journal of Wine Marketing,* 16:3, 14–28

Bijan (2012), Company Homepages, www.bijan.com, www.bijanfragrances.com, Aug 22, 2007

Blanks, Tim, "Die Zukunft des Shoppings hat begonnen: 'Sugoku ii, Armani-san'", *GQ,* Germany, Jan 2008, 188–197

BlingH20 (2012), Company Homepage, www.blingh2o.com, Aug 25, 2012

Boston Common (2012), "9 Gigts in a Bottle", www.bostoncommon-magazine, Internet edition

Bowers & Wilkins (2012), Company Homepage, www.bowers-wilkins.com, Jul 30, 2012

Breguet (2012), Company Homepage, www.breguet.com, Aug 15, 2012

Bristol (2007), Company Homepage, www.bristolcars.co.uk, Nov 4, 2007

Brothers, Caroline (Oct 21–22, 2006): "The precise smell of success", *International Herald Tribune*, 12

Bugatti (2007), Company Homepage, www.bugatti.com, Nov 4, 2007

Business Insider (May 7, 2012), "The 11 Most Expensive Watches Ever Sold", www.businessinsider.com, Internet edition

Businesswire (May 7, 2004), "'New' Luxury Paradigm Shifts to Experience, Says Pam Danziger of Unity Marketing; Old Luxury is about the 'Thing;' New Luxury is the 'Experience'", Internet edition

Capgemini and RBC Wealth Management (2012), "Global High Net Worth Population Increases Slightly as Their Investable Wealth Declines, Finds World Wealth Report", Press Release on *Capgemini.com*, published Jun 19, 2012

Cartier (2006), Company Homepage, www.cartier.com, Oct 22, 2006

Carvajal, Doreen (Sep 30, 2006), "A relentless hunt for the next deal", *International Herald Tribune*, 13

Chien, Yung-Hsin, Edward L. George, Leigh McAlister (2001), "Measuring a Brand's Tendency to be Included in High Value Baskets", *Marketing Letters* 12:4, 287–298

Crossland, Philip and Faye I. Smith (2002), "Value Creation in Fine Arts: A System Dynamics Model of inverse Demand and Information Cascades", *Strategic Management Journal* 23, 417–434

Dabkowski, Colin (Apr 22, 2004), "Research claims standards of beauty based on evolutionary ideals", *Dailyorange.com*, Internet edition

Deeny, Godfrey (Dec 16, 2007), "The Fendi show you could see from space", *Independent Newspaper Ireland*, Internet edition

Delap, Leanne (Oct 27, 2007), "Secret Luxury", *Globe and Mail*, Internet edition

DeMatio, Joe and Georg Kacher (2005): "Porsche Cayman S", *Automobile*, Aug 2005, Internet edition

de Mooij, Marieke, Geert Hofstede (2002), "Convergence and divergence in consumer behavior: implications for international retailing", *Journal of Retailing* 78, 61–69

Dhar, Ravi and Klaus Wertenbroch (2000), "Consumer Choice between Hedonic and Utilitarian Goods", *Journal of Marketing Research* 37, 60–71

Dubois, Bernard and Patrick Duquesne (1993), "The Market for Luxury Goods: Income versus Culture", *European Journal of Marketing* 27,1, 35–44

Dubois, Bernard, Gilles Laurent and Sandor Czellar (2001), "Consumer rapport to luxury: Analyzing complex and ambivalent attitudes,» *Les Cahiers de Recherche 736, Groupe HEC, 56 pages*

Dubois, Bernard, Sandor Czellar and Gilles Laurent (2005), "Consumer Segments Based on Attitudes Toward Luxury: Empirical Evidence from Twenty Countries", *Marketing Letters*, 16:2, 115–128

DuBow, Charles (2008), "The Return of Exclusivity", *BusinessWeek*, February 2008, Internet Edition

Emling, Shelley (Apr 5, 2007), "Fractional Ownership comes to yachting", *International Herald Tribune*, Internet Edition

Encyclopaedia Britannica (2006), www.britannica.com/eb/article-34256, Sep 17, 2006, Internet edition

Encyclopaedia Britannica (2008a), www.britannica.com, Merriam-Webster Collegiate Dictionary and Online Thesaurus, Jan 2, 2008, Internet edition

Encyclopaedia Britannica (2008b), www.britannica.com/eb/article-9068459, Jan 2, 2008, Internet edition

Ferrari (2006), Company Homepage, www.ferrariworld.com, Oct 22, 2006

Forden, Sara Gay: "Luxury-goods makers pursue the richest of the rich", *International Herald Tribune,* Internet edition

Foroohar, Rana (2007), "Luxury Goes Undercover: The best things in life aren't necessarily flashy objects but discreet, meaningful experiences", *Newsweek*, Jul 2, 2007, 46–51

Foulkes, Nick (2007): "For Whatever It's Worth: Luxury companies are always finding ways to get consumers to spend more", *Newsweek*, Jul 2, 2007, 81

Friedmann, Vanessa (Sep 7, 2007), "What Luxury means now", *Financial Times*, Internet edition

Galbraith, Robert (Jun 28, 2006), "New maxim for global luxury brands: Grow and diversify", *International Herald Tribune*, 12

Gentleman, Amelia (Oct 26, 2006), "The flashy cars of a maharajah for modern times", *International Herald Tribune*, 24

Gisquet, Vanessa (2005), "Most Expensive Cosmetics", *Forbes*, Apr 20, 2005, Internet edition

Google (2012), www.google.com, Jul 24, 2012

Guinness, Daphne (Sep 6, 2007), "The conceit of luxury", *The Sydney Morning Herald*, Internet edition

Gulf Times (Sep 2, 2006), "Sports car or bling? Aston Martin debate on luxury, heritage starts", Internet edition

Gumbel, Peter (2007a), "Mass vs. class", *Fortune*, Sep 6, 2007, Internet edition

Gumbel, Peter (2007b), "Luxury goes mass market", *Fortune,* Sep 6, 2007, Internet edition

Guyon, Janet (2004), "The Magic Touch", *Fortune* 150:5, 229–233

Hammonds, Don (Sep 14, 2007), "Bentleys get hotter among rich and famous", *Pittsburgh Post-Gazette*, Internet edition

Hardy, Sam (2008), "Baby Phantom targets Bentley", *Auto Express*, Jan 4, 2008, Internet edition

Harrods (2006), Company Homepage, www.harrods.com, Oct 22, 2006

Hecking, Mirjam (2007a), "Luxusinsel mit 17,5 Knoten", *Manager Magazin*, Mar 19, 2007, Internet edition

Hecking, Mirjam (2007b), "Tickender Mythos", *Manager Magazin*, Sep 17, 2007, Internet edition

Hirschmann, Elizabeth and Morris B. Holbrook (1982), "Hedonic consumption, emerging concepts, methods and propositions", *Journal of Marketing* 46, 92–101

International Herald Tribune (Aug 25, 2006), "Perfect Packaging", Internet edition

International Herald Tribune (Oct 2, 2006), "Super-luxury homes go on the market for $100 million and more", Internet edition

International Herald Tribune (Jun 29, 2007), "Number of millionaires in Asia jumped in 2006", 10

International Herald Tribune (Sep 13, 2007), "€1 million Lamborghinis sell like hotcakes", Internet edition

International Herald Tribune (Sep 23, 2007), "From homemade to Gucci: Booming Vietnam's nouveaux riches indulge a taste for luxury", Internet edition

International Herald Tribune (Oct 26, 2007), "European companies plan to turn Airbus Superjumbo into ultimate executive jet", Internet edition

Jewellery Business (2006): "Watch World – February 2006", www.jewellery-business.com, Feb 2006, Internet edition

Jumeirah (2007): Company Homepage, www.jumeirah.com, Dec 9, 2007

Keefe, Patrick Radden (2007), "The Jefferson Bottles – How could one collector find so much rare fine wine?", *The New Yorker*, Sep 3, 2007, Internet edition

Kemp, Simon (1998), "Perceiving luxury and necessity", *Journal of Economic Psychology* 19, 591–606

Khan, Heena (2012), "Global luxury market moving from products to experience: Survey", The Hindu Business Line, Jun 5, 2012, Internet edition

Kishkovsky, Sophia (Nov 29, 2007), "The Millionaire Fair: Art becomes the next step along the path of riches", *International Herald Tribune*, Internet edition

Kivetz (1999), "Advances in Research on Mental Accounting and Reason-Based Choice", *Marketing Letters,* 10:3, 249–266

Kivetz, Ran and Itamar Simonson (2002a), "Earning the right to indulge: Effort as a Determinant of Customer Preferences towards Frequency Program Rewards", *Journal of Marketing Research* 39:2, 155–170

Kivetz, Ran and Itamar Simonson (2002b), "Self-Control for the Righteous: Toward a Theory of Precommitment to Indulgence", *Journal of Consumer Research* 29:2, 199–217

Kolesnikov, Sonia (Jun 24, 2007): "Relax and Restore: a luxury resort operator takes a conservationist tack", *International Herald Tribune*, Internet edition

La Ferla, Ruth (Sep 13, 2006), "Chic today, gone tomorrow – so why not rent", *International Herald Tribune*, 12

Lageat, Thierry, Sandor Czellar and Gilles Laurent, "Engineering Hedonic Attributes to Generate perceptions of Luxury: Consumer Perception of Everyday Sound", *Marketing Letters* 14:2, 97–109

Lamborghini (2007) "Automobili Lamborghini presents the new Lamborghini Reventón at the IAA 2007 in Frankfurt", Company Press Release, Sep 13, 2007, 4 pages

Lane, Viki R. (2000), "The Impact of Ad Repetition and Ad Content on Consumer Perceptions of Incongruent Extensions", *Journal of Marketing* 64:2, 80–91

Langer, Daniel A. (2008): "The Luxury Formula: Decoding the Hidden Aspects of Luxury and Identifying ist Concept for Profitable Competitive Marketing Strategies", Dissertation, University of Mainz, 463 pages

Langer, Daniel A. and Oliver P. Heil (2013): "Luxury: Marketing & Management", *Amazon (Scottsdale & Mainz)*, 267 pages

Lapenkova, Marina (2007): "Urlaub in der Unterschicht", Spiegel, Nov 8, 2007, Internet edition

Levin, Irvin P., Judy Schreiber, Marco Lauriola, Gary J. Gaeth (2002), "A Tale of Two Pizzas: Building Up from a Basic Product Versus Scaling Down from a Fully Loaded Product", *Marketing Letters* 13:4, 335–344

Lew-Ram, Michal (Dec 20, 2006), "This $310,000 phone blings, then rings", *CNNmoney.com*, Internet edition

Lindner, Melanie (2008), "The Most Outrageously Priced Items", *Forbes*, Feb 8, 2008, Internet edition

Los Angeles Times (Jan 10, 2005), "Hermès May Pose as New Luxury Model", Internet edition

Louis Vuitton (2006), Company Homepage, www.louisvuitton.com, Oct 22, 2006

Louis Vuitton (2007), Company Homepage, www.louisvuitton.com, Dec 9, 2007

Louis Vuitton (2012), Company Homepage, www.louisvuitton.com, Aug 25, 2012

Luxist.com (Jul 13, 2005), "Sam Adams Limited Edition Utopia Beer", Internet edition

Madslien, Jorn (Dec 11, 2007), "Aston to unveil new design centre", *BBC*, Internet edition

Mah, Ann (Sep 19, 2007), "Luxury brands stamped on everything from phones to flowers", *International Herald Tribune*, Internet edition

Maidment, Paul (Sep 18, 2007), "Criminally rich: All the money in the world", *International Herald Tribune*, Internet edition

McGuigan, Cathleen (2007), "A Certain Sense of Calm: Far from the spotlight, a group of gifted architects is designing spaces of quiet elegance", *Newsweek*, Jul 2, 2007, 53–64

McLean, Bethany and Peter Elkind (2003), "The Smartest Guys in the Room: The Amazing Rise and Scandalous Fall of Enron", *Penguin Books (New York)*, 440 pages

Menkes, Suzy (Sep 28, 2004), "Out of Control? Managing Success", *International Herald Tribune*, 11–12

Menkes, Suzy (Dec 11, 2006), "Extreme luxury for the jet set", *International Herald Tribune*, Internet edition

Meyer, Norma (Mar 4, 2007), "Rich man, pour man: Bling H20 sells status by the bottle", *San Diego Newspaper*, Internet edition

Moe, Wendy W., and Peter S. Fader (2001), "Modeling Hedonic Portfolio Products: A joint segmentation Analysis of Compact Disc Sales", *Journal of Marketing Research* 38:3, 376–385

Moore, Booth and Melissa Magsaysay (Aug 19, 2007), "'IT' OR MISS?: This fall, designers are bringing out the heavy artillery", *Los Angeles Times*, Internet edition

Mihalca, Matei (Feb 7, 2005), "Luxury? What it means in China", *Rediff.com*, Internet Edition

Mort, Gillian Sullivan and Trista Rose (2004), "The effect of product type on value linkages in the means-end chain: Implications for theory and method", *Journal of Consumer Behaviour* 3:3, 221–234

Müller, Henrik (Jul 21, 2007), "Neidgesellschaft: Die gelbe Gefahr", *Manager Magazin*, Internet Edition

Nadeau, Barbie (2007), "Luxury Without Labels", *Newsweek*, Jul 2, 2007, 69

Newsweek (2007), "Everything a Men Wants: Tom Ford is back from purgatory and making up his own rules, again", Jul 2, 2007, 73

Nunnally, Jum C. (1978), "Psychometric Theory", *McGraw-Hill (New York)*, 701 pages

O'Curry Suzanne and Michal Strahilevitz (2001), "Probability and Mode of Acquisition Effects on Choices between Hedonic and Utilitarian Options", Marketing Letters, 12:1, 37–49

Ohmae, Kenichi (1982), "The Mind of the Strategist", *McGraw-Hill (New York)*, 320 pages

Okada, Erica Mina (2005), "Justification Effects on Consumer Choice of Hedonic and Utilitarian Goods", Journal of Marketing Research 42:1, 43–53

Passmore, Nick (2003): "World's Most Expensive Wines", *Forbes*, Nov 19, 2003, Internet edition

Patek Philippe (2006), Company Homepage, www.patek.com, Oct 22, 2006

Patek Philippe (2007), Company Homepage, www.patek.com, Sep 22, 2007

Patek Philippe (2012), Company Homepage, www.patel.com, Aug 22, 2012

Pfanner, Eric (Jul 29, 2007): "On Advertising: Luxury gets less flashy", *International Herald Tribune*, Internet edition

Piccione, Michele and Ariel Rubinstein (2006), "Luxury Prices: An Expository Note", Working Paper, *Levine's Bibliography* 122247000000001252, UCLA Department of Economics, 10 pages

Pincus, Jeremy (2004), "The consequence of unmet needs: The evolving role of motivation in consumer research", *Journal of Consumer Behaviour*, 3:4, 375–387

Pitsis, Simone (Jan 2, 2008), "Bearing Marks of distinction", *The Austalian*, Internet edition

Pitzke, Marc (2007), "Nobel-Fitnessclubs: Schwitzende Millionäre", *Manager Magazin*, Jul 19, 2007, Internet edition

Prabhakar, Hitha (2007a), "How Celebs Get Red-Carpet Ready", *Forbes*, Feb 23, 2007, Internet edition

Prabhakar, Hitha (2007b), "World's Most Extravagant Handbags", *Forbes*, Mar 27, 2007, Internet edition

Prabhakar, Hitha and Lauren Sherman (2007), "Hottest New Luxury Watches", *Forbes,* Apr 11, 2007, Internet edition

Pye, Michael (Sep 8, 2007): "Status for sale", *The Scotsman*, Internet edition

Rawsthorn, Alice (Aug 28, 2006), "When the packaging makes it perfect", *International Herald Tribune*, 15

RéVive (2012), Company Homepage, www.reviveskincare.com, Aug 25, 2012

Sharkey, Joe (Oct 17, 2006), "For the super-rich, upgrading means a 787", *International Herald Tribune,* Internet edition

Seeing-stars.com (Sep 22, 2007), "The Ultimate Guide to Celebrities & Hollywood", Internet edition

Simonson, Itamar and Aimee Drolet (2004), "Anchoring Effects on Consumer's Willingness-to-Pay and Willingness-to-Accept", *Journal of Consumer Research* 31:3, 681–690

Spiegel (2007), "Verflickt und zugenäht: Luxuriöseste Handtasche der Welt", Aug 23, 2007, Internet edition

Stuart Weitzman (2007), Company Homepage, www.stuartweitzman.ch, Oct 28, 2007

Sussman, Paul (Dec 1, 2005), "The Ultimate in lingerie: $15m set", *CNN*, Internet edition

Swatch (2008), Company Homepage, www.swatch.com, Feb 16, 2008

Taber, Kimberly Conniff (Oct 10, 2006), "Goo-goo gear?", *International Herald Tribune*, 12

Taylor III, Alex (2006), "Audi: The luxury car brand nobody knows", *Fortune*, Oct 16, 2006, Internet edition

Tesla (2013): Company Homepage, www.teslamotors.com, May 30, 2013

The Economist (Apr 12, 2007), "Italian luxury goods: Tutto in famiglia", Internet edition

The Leading Hotels of the World (2007), Company Homepage, www.lhw.com, Dec 22, 2007

The New Zealand Herald (Oct 20, 2006), "Nokia's luxury model phone a hit in Europe", Internet edition

Thomas, Dana (2007), "Home Shopping Network: Elite clients are not longer heading to the ateliers of top designers for fittings. So the designers are going to them", Newsweek, July 2, 2007, 77

Thomas, Louis and Keith Weigelt (2000), "Product Location Choice and Firm Capabilities: Evidence from the U.S. Automobile Industry", *Strategic Management Journal* 21:9, 897–909

Time Style & Design (2004), "Robert Polet", Fall 2004, Internet edition

Times (Dec 3, 2007), "World's oldest Rolls-Royce most expensive ever", Internet edition

Timpe, Wolfgang (2007), "Captain Future", *GO SIXT* No. 005, Summer 2007, 46–52

Tracey, Brian (no date), "Got money? You'll need a lot to buy this milk", *msnbc.com*, Internet edition

Turner, Sarah (2007), "Millionaires now number 9.5 million, survey finds. Merrill Lynch, Cap Gemini wealth survey shows assets held also up", *Dow Jones Market Watch*, Jun 27, 2007, Internet edition

Vanity Fair (Mar 20, 2007), "Österreichische Leidenschaft", Internet edition

Veevers, Lauren (Oct 15, 2006), "Bentley v Rolls: Battle of the luxury brands", *The Independent,* Internet edition

Vogue (2003), "Will Tom be banned again?", Jan 15, 2003, Internet edition,

Vorasarun, Chanige (2007), "Party Like a Billionaire", *Forbes*, Oct 12, 2007, Internet edition

Wakefield, Kirk L and J Jeffrey Inman (2003), "Situational price sensitivity: the role of consumption occasion, social context and income", *Journal of Retailing* 79, 199–212

Wally (2008), Company Homepage, www.wally.com, Jan 4, 2008

Washington Post (Mar 6, 2005): "Readings", section F03, Internet edition

Watkins, Dinah (2012), "Hunger for Luxury Brands grows ravenously", China Daily, Jun 5, 2012, Internet edition

Weathersby jr, William (2005), "Chanel Ginza", *Architectural Record*, Internet edition, Nov 2005

Weber, Caroline (Aug 26, 2007), "The Devil Sells Prada", *The New York Times*, Internet edition

Westcott, Kathryn (Jan 14, 2008), "Raising a glass to pricey wine", *BBC*, Internet edition

Wikipedia (2012), Online Encyclopedia, http://en.wikipedia.org, Jul 24, 2012

Willis. Andrew (Dec 7, 2007): "This is the Rolls-Royce of watches", *Globe and Mail*, Internet edition

Witchel, Alex (Dec 26, 2007), "Luxury Without the Headache", *The New York Times*, Internet edition

Wüst, Christian (2007): "Pimp my Rolls", *Spiegel*, Dec 22, 2007, Internet edition

Wyllie, Alice (Dec 9, 2006): "Gucci Gucci Coup", *The Scotsman,* Internet edition

Yabroff, Jennie (2007), "Behind the Secret Door", *Newsweek*, Jul 2, 2007, 56

Young, Robb (Nov 23, 2007): "Luxury no longer means loud in Russia", *International Herald Tribune*, Internet edition

Zeithaml, Valarie A. (1988), "Consumer Perceptions of Price, Quality, and Value: A Means-End Model and Synthesis of Evidence", *Journal of Marketing* 52:3, 2–22

www.ingramcontent.com/pod-product-compliance
Lightning Source LLC
Chambersburg PA
CBHW061313220326
41599CB00026B/4857

* 9 7 8 0 6 9 2 3 6 1 2 6 9 *